DEUS VULT

A CONCISE HISTORY OF THE CRUSADES

DEUS VULT

JEM DUDUCU

AMBERLEY

This book is for my parents, who are awesome, and Laura V. and David K. for getting me to put pen to paper. So if you don't like this ... blame them.

First published 2014

Amberley Publishing
The Hill, Stroud
Gloucestershire, GL5 4EP

www.amberley-books.com

British Library Cataloguing in Publication Data.
A catalogue record for this book is available from the British Library.

ISBN 978-1-4456-4055-6 (paperback)
ISBN 978-1-4456-4088-4 (ebook)

Typeset in 10pt on 13pt Sabon.
Typesetting and Origination by Fakenham Prepress Solutions.
Printed in the UK.

Contents

Introduction   9

1 The Real Beginning of the Crusades: From Jesus
to 1095   13

2 Pope Urban II's Armed Pilgrimage: The First
Crusade   33

3 A New Type of Crusade: The Second Crusade
and the Rise of Saladin   59

4 Legends Are Born: The Third Crusade   95

5 War Crimes: The Fourth Crusade   106

6 Heresy: The Albigensian Crusade in France   120

7 The Crusades Go to Egypt: The Fifth Crusade
and the Changing Nature of the Crusading
Movement   138

8 Blood and Snow: The Northern Crusades   146

9 Prester John: The Sixth Crusade and the Storm
from the East   153

10 To Egypt ... Again: The Seventh Crusade   165

11 They're Back! More Mongolian Mayhem and
the Rise of the Mamelukes, 1256–70   176

12 The End Game, 1270–91   187

13 Betrayal: Final Crusading Plans and the
Templar 'Heresy'   206

Conclusion   221

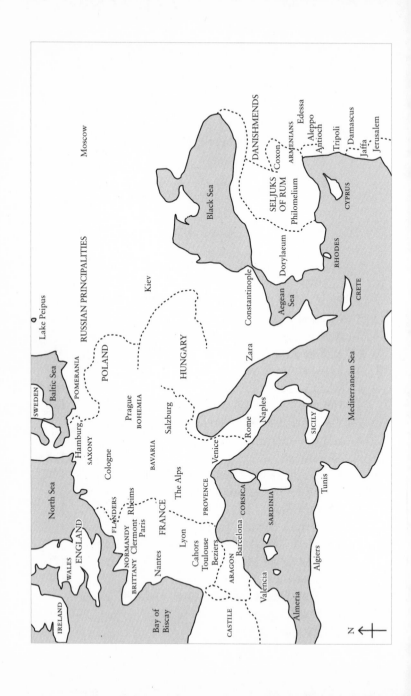

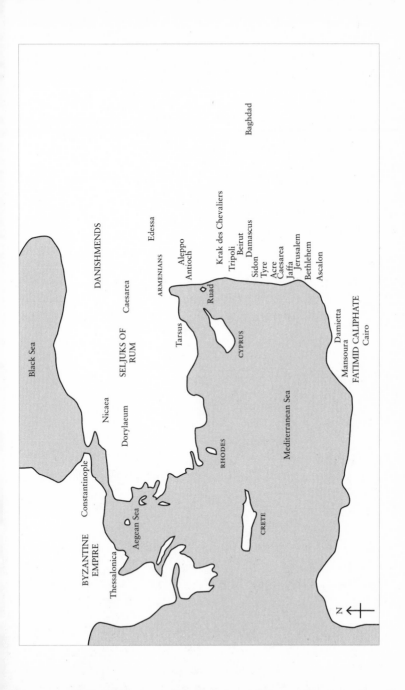

Introduction

When I was doing my degree in the 1990s, there was no historical topic considered to be mustier, more obscure, more self-indulgent than the Crusades. After all, what relevance did medieval wars have to the modern world? Even Pope John Paul II apologised for them, showing them to be something best forgotten, even by the organisation that started and nurtured them.

All that changed on 11 September 2001, when Islamic extremists attacked the United States of America in a series of spectacular acts of suicidal violence and destruction. These events changed everything and led directly to two major wars on the other side of the world. They also prompted questions about where the hatred originated.

It may surprise many readers to learn that in the Middle East people still talk about the Crusades as if these events had happened only yesterday. What has been forgotten in the West is still alive in the minds of millions of Muslims.

In the West the word 'crusade' has been used in recent times to convey a noble concept. There were crusades on litter and crusades on crime. It didn't mean that people were trying to carry out war crimes; it meant that they wanted to do the right thing for the common good.

One example of the West's image of the Crusades as pure and noble adventures can be summarised by the opening words of the letter General Eisenhower circulated to the Allied troops prior to D-Day:

> Soldiers, Sailors and Airmen of the Allied Expeditionary Force! You are about to embark upon a great crusade, toward which we have striven these many months.

A similar statement post 9/11 by a Western general would be unthinkable.

9/11 changed the game and an area of history that had once seen a calm, intellectual, academic look at the Crusades and events in the Middle East and in Europe in the Middle Ages turned into rallying cries of justification by both political groups and religious extremists on all sides. Yes, the Middle East remembered the Crusades, but its people and their leaders also nursed grudges over much more recent history.

But being angry about events that happened centuries ago won't change them. The Crusades were not a brief or obscure moment in history. They shaped the religious and political landscapes of many countries over centuries, which is why it's important to look objectively and unemotionally at the past in order to understand contemporary events.

Just before 9/11, the British film director Guy Ritchie was planning a movie about the Siege of Malta and wanted to call it *Jihad*. If this sounds like box-office poison to you now, it's a sign of how much things changed in Western society in just one day in 2001. The film was never made, which is a shame because the siege would make a cracking movie.

I am, of course, writing in an area where there are many masterful works on the subject (but as you will see, I don't believe they start or end in the right places). I will mention them now as I will be referring to them as I go along. If you read my first book, *The Busy Person's Guide to British*

History, you know I do things a little differently. For a start, you are reading an introduction, which many history books omit; they assume prior knowledge and/or that the work will be read by academics. I try to make no such assumptions. Secondly, who reads those footnotes or the last twenty pages of bibliography? Honestly? If you want to fact check, there's always the internet; but if this book has inspired you to look more closely at this fascinating chapter in history, then here are the 'big boys', which I have referenced when memory failed.

Recent books:
Jerusalem: The Biography by Simon Sebag Montefiore
The Popes: A History by John Julius Norwich
God's War by Christopher Tyerman

Some interesting reading on specific topics:
The Trial of the Templars by Malcolm Barber
The Byzantine Empire by Robert Browning
The Kingdom of Cyprus and the Crusades 1191–1374 by Peter W. Edbury

Then there are the classics:
The two-volume *A History of the Crusades* by Steven Runciman
The Crusades by Hans Eberhard Mayer (best name on the list)

If I genuinely didn't think I could add anything to this amazing canon of texts, I wouldn't have bothered with my own. Most of these are rather learned tomes and will explain events in great depth. But I'd like to think I might win in the 'Interesting Tour Guide' stakes. I would also point out that most of the general books on the topic miss an important truth: the Crusades didn't just happen in the

Middle East, and the more obscure crusading endeavours ironically turned out to be among the most successful.

For a historian specialising in this era, this book is not for you. It's my attempt to put more than 300 years of religious wars that stretched across three continents into an easily digestible format for the casual reader. Got that? Good, then let us begin this fascinating and bloody journey ...

1

The Real Beginning of the Crusades: From Jesus to 1095

In 1095 Pope Urban II, in the French town of Claremont, electrified western Europe with an idea, a revolutionary idea that was to mould Western thinking for centuries. The idea could be summarised as: 'God will reward you if you fight to achieve His goals.'

The speech in Claremont would lead to the expedition that would eventually be known as 'The First Crusade' (1096–99); and inevitably, it is where almost all books on the Crusades start. Urban's speech was sensational and would start the chain of events that would send thousands of Christian knights on a journey across Continental Europe to do battle in the Holy Land against 'the infidel'. But this is not where the story should start.

Instead, let us rewind the clock to more than 1,000 years before Urban, to another continent, to the very source of Christianity, to Jesus. Whether you are a Christian or not is irrelevant. Even a passing knowledge of Jesus (fact: Jesus is Greek translation of the Hebrew name Yeshua or Joshua, so if all names in the Bible should be standardised, he should be known as Joshua) will reveal he was clearly a man of peace. Whether you believe he is part of the Holy Trinity, or a prophet or a wise man, there can be no doubt that his preaching was inclusive and avoided violent imagery or threats. Some of his most famous quotes recorded in the Gospels are the phrases:

Love your neighbour as yourself.

Mark 12:31

Whoever slaps you on the right cheek turn the other.

Matthew 5:39

As you wish that others would do to you, do so to them.

Luke 6:31

In short, had Christian society held those teachings close to its heart and behaved accordingly, Urban's call to arms in the name of the Lord would have fallen on deaf ears.

So how did the idea of 'Holy War' develop?

The first few centuries of Christianity were the epitome of peaceful adherence to the teachings of Jesus. There were no wars declared in his name and no massacres of the followers of opposing ideologies. However, all this changed because of one man named Flavius Aurelius Constantinus Augustus. You will know him better as the Emperor Constantine.

Born in modern-day Serbia to a general of the Roman Empire, Constantine was to have as much impact on Christianity as Jesus himself. Indeed, his influence was so great that we cannot be sure what Christianity would look like today if he hadn't come to power.

By the early fourth century the Roman Empire had a number of emperors and sub-emperors running things. By and large, the system worked and overcame the problems of distance. If there was a rebellion in Asia Minor (Turkey) and the emperor was in Gaul (France), then it could take a year to gather an army and respond. With the system of sub-emperors, local problems could be solved locally.

One of these sub-emperors was Constantius, Constantine's

father, who was reunited with his son in York, where they campaigned together against the Pictish tribes beyond Hadrian's Wall. Before dying in 306, Constantius demanded his son take over his position. This worked until 311, when low-key power playing turned into full-blown civil war between Constantine and the Western Emperor, Maxentius.

In 312 Constantine invaded northern Italy, and, after a series of spectacular successes, moved on Rome. Maxentius was not unduly alarmed; he had the larger army and Rome was well prepared and provisioned for a siege. Constantine could ravage the countryside all he wanted, but he was unlikely to get at Maxentius himself.

However, Maxentius's preparation for a siege was seen as cowardice by the people of Rome, and they taunted him into brash action.

In the summer of 312 Maxentius built a bridge over the Tiber and assembled a huge army. Including his elite Praetorian Guard, the force was twice the size of Constantine's. Maxentius moved his troops over the Milvian Bridge and positioned his men with their backs to the river. Tactically, this was risky because if anything went wrong there was nowhere the army could go. But he had more of everything. With his elite troops at his side, what could go wrong?

Several sources say that Constantine had a vision of Jesus before the battle, and subsequently made all his troops wear the mark of the chi-rho (an X with a P superimposed; these two letters are the first two letters of 'Christ' in Greek). He also had a banner with Jesus' image made. When battle commenced, the unusual symbols on the Roman shields confused Maxentius's troops. With the banner held aloft, Jesus appeared to come from nowhere, so that Maxentius's troops were thrown into disarray.

The Christian iconography had given Constantine the edge. The battle was over very quickly because Maxentius's troops had nowhere to retreat, so both he and the cream of his army drowned as they attempted to get across the river. Constantine's victory was complete, and a few days later Maxentius's body was fished out of the Tiber and beheaded, for good measure.

The Battle of the Milvian Bridge is seen as the first Christian military victory in history. But like most things in life, it wasn't that simple. This battle was not Christians versus pagans; there would have been Christians on both sides. Also, both leaders were pagan, and while the use of Christian iconography did prove decisive in the battle, had it not been used it was still likely that Constantine would have eventually won the day. However, if you want to start talking about the influence of Jesus in wars, the conversation undeniably starts with this battle.

Certainly as the years passed and the memories of Constantine the man faded, he became an important example of muscular Christianity. He is often referred to in late antiquity and the medieval era in this context. He's a devout Christian, a holy warrior and is, of course, a saint. Yet he did not convert until he was dying. If Jesus had blessed him with victory and a powerful reign, he didn't acknowledge it until the very end of his days (he was baptised on his deathbed). So this most 'Christian' of rulers was actually as pagan as Julius Caesar. His triumphal arch, built to commemorate the Battle of the Milvian Bridge, had typical Roman pagan iconography on it. Jesus was nowhere to be seen.

Constantine was the most influential pagan in Christianity. For the time being he and the Eastern Emperor, Licinius, allowed free religious expression throughout the empire. This was to remain the status quo for a decade, but this was not the same thing as having a Christian empire. Christians were still in the minority but didn't fear any oppression. However, as a sign that Licinius was testing his western counterpart, he started bullying Christians from 320 onwards. There was no bloody massacre (showing how, by the 320s, Christians were too well ensconced in Roman society to be victimised); it was more a case of high-profile Christians in the East losing their jobs or having lands and funds confiscated.

This was a challenge to Constantine and in 324 there was another civil war. Constantine again used Christian iconography and preaching to boost the morale of his men; and as Licinius was using pagan Goth mercenaries to bolster his forces, this conflict was far easier to divide on Christian versus pagan lines. Licinius lost a string of battles, which led to his downfall. Then, even though Constantine gave him an easy opt-out (anything for a quiet life), Licinius continued scheming, leaving Constantine no option but to have him executed (and, in addition, also had his son murdered – just to be sure).

For the first time in generations, the entire Roman Empire was now under the immediate jurisdiction of just one man. Constantine realised he needed a glue to hold all the nations of the empire together, and as Christianity had brought him many victories, he made it the official religion of the empire. That's not to say that everyone happily gave up old beliefs to become Christian; but Christianity was now out of the shadows, in the ascendancy and never again marginalised in the empire.

To show this kind of recasting of the empire, Constantine looked around for a new capital city. He chose the small but recently rebuilt Greek city of Byzantium and renamed it Constantinople. He filled it with as many Christian holy relics as possible, including the True Cross (supposedly genuine remnants of the cross on which Jesus was crucified). This city became integral to Christian history, also becoming a focus of the Crusades – and the ultimate prize for Muslims, too.

His interest in holy Christian shrines stretched to the city most associated with Jesus' preaching, Jerusalem. It was here that Constantine's own mother claimed to have found Jesus' tomb, and a magnificent church, the Church of the Holy Sepulchre, was built around it. Was it really Jesus' tomb? To the modern eye the evidence is flimsy at best. It's worth remembering that, between Jesus' death and the age of Constantine, the city had been razed to the ground and left as wilderness for generations before slowly being rebuilt.

However, Constantine's greatest contribution to Christianity is not measured in buildings or battles, but in the Council of Nicaea in 325. This council was pivotal in agreeing so much that has become standard in Christianity.

First of all, it sorted out the Bible. Prior to Constantine's reign, Christians had a plethora of materials to refer to. Apart from the Gospels of Matthew, Mark, Luke and John, there were a number of others, most famously the Gospel according to St Thomas and the Gospel according to St Judas. Why are there only four Gospels in the New Testament? The simple answer is because the Council of Nicaea said so. The Book of Revelations is quite ... challenging. How did that get into the Bible? The answer is that it very nearly didn't make the cut, but the council again thought it should be an essential document.

Most of the formula of modern Christianity was devised in Asia Minor in 325, by a group of men who never met Jesus and lived hundreds of years later in a different country. Was this what Jesus had in mind? The answer is 'we'll never know', but chances are, probably not. The council also formalised the calculation of the date of Easter and Jesus' relationship to God. Until this point it had been openly debated whether Jesus was a prophet loved by God, or part of a Holy Trinity. This may sound odd to modern Christians, but that's because contemporary beliefs were solidified, ratified and authorised at the Council of Nicaea.

This was a meeting of most of the great churchmen of the day, supervised and ordered by the pagan Constantine, who had his own less than spiritual agenda: get agreement, then the 'official' version could be spread throughout the empire, ensuring its cohesion.

By the time of his death in 337, Constantine could easily be considered one of the greatest Roman emperors; in fact, one of the most important people in history. His elevation of Christianity to the core of a mature empire was to have consequences that still echo today.

Under Constantine and innumerable kings, queens and emperors to come, Christianity had military muscle, something the faith had never had before. At the Milvian Bridge, Jesus had been called upon like Ares or Mars had in the past, and he had delivered victory. It came at exactly the right time, too, because just a few generations later the Western Empire was under serious threat from pagan armies.

And it was at this time, in the early fifth century, that Saint Augustine wrote the *City of God*. In it he coins the term 'just war' and points out that

> the commandment forbidding killing is not broken by those
> who have waged wars on the authority of God.

The idea of having divine backing in a war was nothing new. The Old Testament is full of battles where God gave the Israelites victory or smote the Jews for their wickedness and noncompliance. Going beyond the realms of the Bible, the Persians called on Ahura Mazda, the Greeks on Nike or Artemis, and the Egyptians on Horus. Having a god of war or a god backing their military campaigns was a way of explaining defeat or victory.

What was new was Christian theologians using a philosophical sleight of hand to justify actions that specifically went against some of Jesus' key teachings. Ultimately, 'offering the other cheek' works fine on an individual level, but no country can survive with that as its foreign policy. Saint Augustine's work was extremely influential and came at a time when the Western Roman Empire was in its long-drawn-out death throes. Now Christian armies had a moral mandate to defend their lands from aggressive pagan expansion. For a time, entire countries were lost to Christendom. The outlook was grim.

In the East, however, the empire thrived. Its high point came under Emperor Justinian (527–65), who reinvigorated the Eastern Empire and even reclaimed significant areas of the Western one, too. His capital was, of course, Constantinople, where he built the Hagia Sophia, which was the largest cathedral in the world for nearly 1,000 years, a title that no other building can claim.

Justinian had temporarily stopped the rot, but it was another Eastern Roman (Byzantine) emperor who played a key role in the story of the Crusades. Heraclius was emperor from 610 to 641, and his story doesn't start well. In 611 those age-old enemies of the Romans, the Persians, were once more on the march. They had spectacular success, capturing modern-day Georgia and Syria, with a spearhead into Anatolia. Byzantium was on its knees, but in 613 Heraclius brought together a defence force and met them at Antioch ... where he was roundly defeated. Disaster turned to catastrophe. Jerusalem fell to the Persians, who then invaded Egypt, the breadbasket of the empire. Meanwhile, with Heraclius so weakened, the Slavs in the Balkans advanced on Constantinople itself. It really should have been game over for both emperor and empire.

It was as Heraclius despaired that the Patriarch of Constantinople (the religious high authority of the empire), Sergius, calmed his nerves and offered to use Church funds to buy the way to peace and to rebuild the army.

Safe behind the walls of Constantinople, Heraclius was able to sue for peace with the Persians in exchange for an annual tribute of 1,000 talents of gold, 1,000 talents of silver, 1,000 silk robes, 1,000 horses and 1,000 virgins (that's a lot of virgins). The peace gave him the breathing space he so desperately needed and allowed him to rebuild the empire's army by slashing non-military expenditure, devaluing the currency and melting down (with Sergius's approval) Church treasures to raise the necessary funds to continue the war.

Heraclius assembled his forces in Asia Minor and revived the morale of the troops by explaining the new phase of the conflict in religious terms. They were not just trying to defeat the enemies of the empire, but the enemies of God. These pagans had captured the Holy City of Jerusalem, and the Christians were on a mission from God to recover it and crush the Persian threat, once and for all. The entire character of the campaign was framed by the concept of Holy War. It already had the backing of the Church, but now an *acheiropoietos* (meaning miraculous or not made by man) image of Christ was carried as a military standard. They were officially on a mission from God, paid for by God (well, the Church), with God on their side. The religious imperative makes this, in many ways, the first 'crusade'.

And it looked like God was, undeniably, on their side because from this point onwards they never lost against the Persians. The Roman army proceeded to Armenia, inflicted defeat on an army led by a Persian-allied Arab chief, and then won a victory over the main Persian army. Heraclius would stay on campaign for several years. But while the main Byzantine forces were focused in Asia, in 626 the Slavs, supported by the Persian army, besieged Constantinople. The siege ended in failure, and the victory was attributed to the icons of the Virgin, which were led in procession by Sergius around the walls of the city. At the same time a second Persian army suffered another crushing defeat at the hands of Heraclius's brother, Theodore. This remarkable change in fortunes could only be attributed to God's blessing.

In 627, with the Persian war effort disintegrating, Heraclius launched a winter offensive into Mesopotamia, where he defeated the Persians at the Battle of Nineveh. Continuing south along the Tigris, he sacked the great palace at Dastagird. Discredited by this series of disasters, the Persian Shahenshah (King of Kings) Khosrau was overthrown and killed in a coup led by his son, who at once sued for peace, agreeing to withdraw from all occupied territories. In 629 Heraclius restored the True Cross to Jerusalem in a majestic ceremony.

The Persian Empire had been a global player for a millennium, and it now lay in tatters. Persia would rise again, but this turned out to be the last act of the old Zoroastrian Persia. It would be rebuilt, not in the image of Darius and Xerxes of old, but under a new influence – Islam.

This was the end result of what should be known as the First Crusade, or at least, the First Holy War. It had a leader motivated by the realities on the ground, but able to frame the war in a religious context. He was supported both spiritually and financially by the Church, where one of the key aims of the war was the recapture of Jerusalem. Putting it another way, there's nothing about Heraclius's campaign that didn't qualify it as a crusade.

After his victory over Persia, Heraclius took the ancient Persian title of 'King of Kings'. Later on, starting in 629, he styled himself as Basileus, the Greek word for 'sovereign', and that title was used by all the Byzantine emperors for the next 800 years. Heraclius's defeat of the Persians ended a war that had been going on, intermittently, for almost 400 years and left the Persian Empire in disarray, a state from which it never recovered.

So Heraclius achieved the total victory over the Persians that had eluded all the great emperors of the past. This religious mandate and success in war is thought to have had an impact on one of Heraclius's contemporaries further south, the Prophet Muhammad. Sadly for Heraclius, no sooner had he settled old scores than a brand-new threat emerged in the form of a group of Arabs called 'Muslims'. They exploded out of the Arabian Peninsula and engulfed most of the Byzantine territory in the Middle East. Before Heraclius died, he saw all his hard campaigning undone by a threat he could never have foreseen.

Heraclius is important for inventing the religious war (it's debatable whether the Prophet was directly influenced by it, but Heraclius is the only Roman emperor indirectly referred to in the Qur'an, the Muslim holy book; but regardless, his religious war predates the jihad of the caliphate). Further, he sat astride the world both as it had been for a thousand years and as it would be for the next thousand years. The Persians had been a threat as far back as the Battle of Marathon, and he had finished them off. Although the rise of Islam would lead to a number of different Muslim dynasties, all would challenge the West for supremacy.

A proper explanation of the Crusades cannot be told purely from a western Christian point of view. As Heraclius's story clearly shows, the history of the early Islamic caliphate must be understood, too.

The Prophet Muhammad was roughly a contemporary of Heraclius and began his career as a trader. Some revisionist historians have pointed out that none of the sources for Muhammad are contemporary. While this is correct, the fact that he fought battles, founded lasting societies and even had a flesh and blood family means that far more is known about him than about Jesus.

The Qu'ran, unlike the Bible, was not created over many centuries by many writers, but was dictated to Muhammad by the Angel Gabriel (yes, the same one who spoke to Mary) in powerful visions. As always, new beliefs find their followers and critics, too. In 622, because the situation was becoming positively dangerous, Muhammad was forced to flee Mecca for Medina. This journey (*Hijra*) marks the start of the Islamic calendar. From Medina, Muhammad led his believers for another ten years, before dying of fever.

From a historical perspective, Muhammad's greatest achievement was to unify a disparate group of tribes under one banner. In his own lifetime the Arabian Peninsula transformed from an area of internecine tribal warfare to the epicentre of this new belief. After the Prophet's death, his followers exploded out of that region and across the known world. It was their divine right to conquer and they did so with ferocity in battle, but calmness in conquest. This was not the time of great massacres.

Some Christians believe that a prime indicator that their faith is 'the one truth faith' lies in the fact that just 100 years after Jesus's crucifixion there were Christian communities to be found all over the Roman Empire. This is true, but if that's the measure of a faith's validity, then they should be Muslims because 100 years after the death of Muhammad the Umayyad Caliphate stretched from modern-day Pakistan to Spain. And these weren't just pockets of believers. From a Christian perspective, these were key lands and centres of learning that were lost forever to Islam. For example, in the fourth century, Egypt was an important centre of Christian thought and debate. By 700 it had become an important area in the Islamic Caliphate, and to this day only 5 per cent of the country is Christian.

In 636 Abu Ubaidah (one of the companions of Muhammad) achieved a spectacular victory when he successfully besieged Jerusalem. It fell in 637 and this was followed by an undramatic change of government and very little disruption to the city itself. Now the Muslims ruled the third most holy city in their religion (although for a time Muslims prayed towards Jerusalem, not Mecca) and became the custodians of the most holy sites for the two other monotheistic religions. Until the latter half of the twentieth century (with only a short crusader interlude – much more on that later), Jerusalem was a Muslim city.

In 691 the Umayyad Caliph Abd al-Malik firmly imprinted an Islamic statement on the holiness of Jerusalem with the creation of the Dome of the Rock. This building is unique in that it is the only 'holy' Muslim building in the world which is not a mosque. It covers the rock where Muhammad is supposed to have risen to heaven to meet God, Jesus and all the prophets of the Old Testament. The location itself was chosen because at the time it was little more than a spoil heap, one of the few disused areas of the city. However, it was also the site of the Temple of Solomon, and while it was not then a location of pilgrimage for Jews, the one standing wall (now called the Wailing Wall) would many centuries later become a focal point for Jews, thus creating a completely unsolvable religious conundrum.

The Dome of the Rock does seem to have some kind of footprint indentation; however, before the time of Abd al-Malik, this holy rock's features had been attributed to Jesus and, even earlier, to Jewish religious figures. In short, the Muslims were continuing the common tradition of inheriting something of religious significance and explaining it within their own framework.

Opposite the Dome is the Al-Aqsa mosque, which to the modern eye doesn't look like a mosque. That's because the rulers of the time wanted to build a new place of worship suited to its prize location. The very best architects were Byzantine, so they used the same basic guidelines that would be used for building an Orthodox church. And this is why a fine, bespoke and very ancient Muslim place of worship looks like it could be a converted late antiquity church.

By the end of the same year (637), the Muslim armies had gone as far north as Antioch and successfully captured that, too. Now the Byzantine Empire would be a rump of its former glory, never again stretching further east than the modern-day borders of eastern Turkey.

The expansion of Islam continued west across North Africa and, a couple of generations later, was staring across the narrow straits of the entrance to the western Mediterranean. Spain, which had been a Romano-Christian stronghold, had suffered for centuries from invasions of pagan barbarians, but had been reclaimed as a Christian area in the late sixth century. This success was turned into despair in 711, when Muslim Berbers from North Africa invaded. By 717 the Iberian Peninsula was under Muslim control; and it was only at the Battle of Tours in 732 that a small Frankish army, led by Charles Martel ('the Hammer'), stopped the Muslim conquest of France. The Battle of Tours was the high tide of the western expansion of Islam thanks to Charles and his successors, who managed to keep it south of the Pyrenees.

The years 600–1000 in Europe were terrible times. As already mentioned, Christian lands at the start of this period were falling to a new religion at an alarming rate. But it didn't stop there. From the east, the Magyars – horsemen riding in from the Asian steppes – came pillaging and plundering. From the north, there was the hit-and-run destruction characteristic of those most pagan of people, the Vikings. The Christian British Isles were in the unique and terrifying position of having been invaded after the fall of Rome by pagan Angles, Jutes and Saxons. It took centuries to Christianise characteristic them, only to have these Christian Anglo-Saxons invaded by a new wave of Viking pagans.

There were bright spots: Pope (and later Saint) Gregory

the Great sent Christian missionaries to faraway lands. Charlemagne (Charles Martel's grandson) united what was left of Christian mainland Europe. But these were flickers of hope in an otherwise grim time. By now St Augustine's idea of a 'just war' was both proven and practical. What wasn't 'just' about defending your lands from Vikings, whose mission was to rob, burn and murder? These murderous pagans proved to all onlookers that Christianity created a far more peaceable society than did the beliefs of these warlike peoples. Things in Europe were desperate.

Not so for the caliphate. Over time the original empire would suffer civil war and break up; but in the meantime, Islam was thriving and there was an explosion of Islamic learning. Poetry, science, mathematics, philosophy, astronomy, medicine and history all flourished in the Islamic centres of Alexandria, Baghdad and Cordoba. Indeed, it was at this the point that the Muslim east completely eclipsed the Christian west in terms of knowledge. For example, the Romans had never used the mathematical value of 0. When it did get transported to Europe, the Church feared and banned it for centuries, for a null value was a void, and the void is where the Devil dwells. 0 was a potentially dangerous number! So the Indian symbol used to describe this value is 'zero', which is an Arabic word.

And it doesn't end there. Our entire numerical system is based on the Arab one. While the Romans get a lot of credit for introducing many concepts to Western society, their understanding and use of mathematics was unwieldy at best. To illustrate: the number 1973 in Roman numerals is MCMLXXIII. The Islamic system allowed, for the first time, the mastery of complex mathematics and large numbers.

It's a little-known fact that the great Hellenic works of Socrates, Plato and others are preserved not from the original Greek but from Islamic translations of the originals. Many scientific words in English have Arabic roots: cipher, algebra, alchemy and even alcohol. The Muslim world was doing well in trade and science, with its lingua franca of Arabic. By comparison, the West had a long way to go.

Before we can come to Urban's famous speech, there is just one more piece of the jigsaw to fall into place, and that piece belongs to a group that will forever be known as 'the Turks'.

For a thousand years from roughly 400 to 1400, every 200 years or so, something happened in the Central Asian steppes to cause a group of nomads to head west. This connection in geography, ethnicity, culture and society has incorrectly led the modern Republic of Turkey to group them together as 'Turkish Empires'. While it is correct that the Huns were in many ways like the Magyars or the Turks, the reality is that they were no more closely related than France and Germany – and those two countries aren't exactly big on brotherly love.

'Turks' is a general word and a phrase mostly used outside that society. For example, in the West you hear references to the 'Ottoman Turks', but the sultans recognised that they ruled a polyglot nation and referred to the whole of humanity within their borders as 'Ottomans', within which there would be subdivisions of ethnicity, such as Greeks or Syrians. The generalisations go the other way too, as throughout the crusading era in the Middle East the Islamic chronicles lump all of western Europe together as 'Franks'.

However, by the turn of the first millennium, nomadic horsemen began to raid on the edges of the Byzantine and Islamic worlds. Some raiders were hostile, some could be bought and used as mercenaries, and others disappeared just as quickly as they arrived. The story of the early Seljuk Turks exists on the very fringes of history; and it's interesting that, at a time when so much writing and learning was going on in cities like Constantinople and Baghdad, very little was known about these nomadic peoples.

The year 1071 is the first important date in Seljuk history, the year of the Battle of Manzikert. The Byzantine Emperor, Romanos IV Diogenes, was well aware that a threat was coming, so he hired some of the meanest mercenaries in the world to bolster his considerable home-grown forces. The Normans were at their apogee of martial efficiency in the 1070s, so they were also hired. Then there was the legendary Varangian Guard, made up of Anglo-Saxon Englishmen and Vikings, who wore steel helmets and long suits of mail armour, and who carried huge, two-handed battleaxes capable of cleaving a man from shoulder to waist in one blow. It is intriguing to think that both veterans and enemies of 1066 (Vikings, English and Normans) were potentially all fighting on the same side.

Romanos sought to fight fire with fire and had his own detachment of mercenary Seljuk horse archers. He had done everything right. He had mustered an army of about 50,000 (to put this into some perspective, at the Battle of Hastings neither side fielded a force of more than 7,000) and was ready to face Alp Arslan, the fierce warlord of the Seljuks. All Romanos had to do was find him.

Anatolia in summer is like an oven, and Romanos had to cover hundreds of miles with a ponderously slow army. He didn't help matters by bringing a baggage train packed with luxuries and imperial comforts, which led to grumbling from the foot soldiers. And as usual, this Western force lived off the land, meaning that the imperial army plundered whatever they needed, which led to hatred and bitterness on the part of the local population.

Despite advice to hold in a key position, Romanos wanted to find this Seljuk army and end the Turkish incursions once and for all. Desperate to locate Alp Arslan, Romanos split the army in two and sent half off with his trusted and experienced general Tarchaneiotes. This was risky. Splitting a force is rarely advisable, but both armies were large and – in theory – more than capable of defending themselves.

Towards the end of August, Romanos arrived in Manzikert to find it empty of all troops. Had the battle already been won by his general? There was no time to find out as the familiar raids from the horse archers began again. Romanos sent out a detachment of cavalry to locate the source of these incursions, which resulted in the discovery of the entire Turkish force. Most of the cavalry was either killed or captured. As the skirmishing continued, Romanos must have wondered what had happened to his general.

When the two main forces finally met, it was obvious that Alp Arslan's army was considerable. By the 1070s the Seljuks had converted to Islam, which gave them access to diplomatic channels and, ultimately, troops from the major Muslim cities of the East. These weren't just Turks, but also Syrians from Aleppo, among other allies. Alp Arslan sent envoys to talk peace, but Romanos wasn't interested. He knew he had everything to lose if he didn't stop the Seljuks now.

Worse was still to come. Many of Romanos's Turkic mercenaries felt they had more in common with Alp Arslan's forces than with the Byzantine army. On the morning of the battle, Romanos awoke to discover many had switched sides.

On 26 August 1071, Romanos led what remained of his army (still of a considerable size) against Alp Arslan. A number of key things happened, almost all of them at the start of the battle. Firstly, if Romanos was hoping for Tarchaneiotes to arrive on the field of battle, he was bitterly disappointed. His general had already been engaged by the Muslim army and crushed – no help was coming.

Secondly, as soon as battle was ordered, the sizeable Norman mercenary contingent simply refused to fight.

The Normans were not cowards, but they were shrewd and knew a lost cause when they saw one. That said, their withdrawal didn't help the situation.

Finally, Alp Arslan's strategy was the tried and tested (and eventually legendary) tactic of using the shape of the crescent for his horse archers. As Romanos advanced, the Turkish centre would slowly retreat. Meanwhile, the wings of the Seljuk forces would creep around the flanks of the enemy in an attempt to surround them, all the time pouring arrow fire into the sides of the enemy troops. It didn't always work, but on this occasion it was textbook.

Romanos's forces were shattered and the fighting, while long and bloody (with the Varangian Guard bravely defending the emperor in a last stand), did little to affect the ultimate outcome. It was a crushing defeat for Byzantium that would forever allow a Turkish presence in Anatolia.

The emperor was captured by his mortal enemy. Alp Arslan put his foot on Romanos's neck and forced him to kiss the earth. He then raised the exhausted and blood-spattered emperor to his feet and asked him, 'What would you do, if I was brought before you as a prisoner?'

There must have been a tense moment as Romanos thought what to say. The next words out of his mouth could well be his last.

'Perhaps I'd kill you, or march you through the streets of Constantinople,' he replied.

'My punishment is far heavier. I forgive you and set you free,' said Alp Arslan.

As a peace treaty and ransom were negotiated, Romanos ate at Alp Arslan's side, but his comment was prophetic. When Romanos did return to Byzantine lands, he was forced into a civil war and was eventually blinded and deposed, his subjects treating him with less kindness than his enemy.

It is vital to understand that this defeat for the Byzantine

Empire was to start the gradual and permanent transition of eastern Anatolia into a Muslim and Turkic area. However, it was still under fairly recent new ownership when the First Crusade marched through the area just a generation later.

2

Pope Urban II's Armed Pilgrimage: The First Crusade

The first chapter covered over a thousand years of human history, so you will be pleased to hear that events will now slow down to a more leisurely pace.

While Alp Arslan died at the hands of assassins in 1072, his trusted general Atsiz had been ordered south. He descended on Jerusalem and starved it into submission. Being a relatively new convert to Islam himself, he had a deep respect for this holy city.

However, once Jerusalem surrendered, he marched on Egypt, where he overextended his lines. He was defeated and retreated back towards the holy city. Unfortunately news of his defeat reached the population before he did, and he faced rebellion. He was a Turk and Turks don't take betrayal lightly. His piety evaporated. A gate was left open for him, and he and his remaining army poured in, taking out their anger and frustration on the inhabitants. It was the worst massacre the city had seen for many generations. Muslims, Jews and Christians all faced his wrath; the butchery was not religiously motivated – this was revenge. He was an equal opportunity slaughterer.

When the news of this massacre reached Europe, the story centred on Christian fatalities, rather than on the more nuanced fact that a city had rebelled and the warlord had exacted his revenge on the population as a whole; the Christian pilgrims had not been specifically singled out. However, this wasn't the only report of a Christian massacre at the time. In an entirely unrelated episode in 1064, 5,000 German and Dutch pilgrims were massacred by Bedouins.

Since the roads to Jerusalem were, by and large, considered to be safe for Christian travellers to the Holy Land, pilgrims always marched unarmed and had been doing so for centuries. It should be noted that at this point Jerusalem had been under Muslim rule for more than 400 years, with little hostility aimed at Christian pilgrims. However there had now been two massacres in the space of a decade. Surely something needed to be done about this!

Quite often, Catholic apologists point to these two massacres as key triggers to Urban's speech at Claremont. It's sleight of hand, implying that the Muslims started it and that Pope Urban wasn't that bellicose. While any kind of massacre is abhorrent, this is a tough sell because there was no such preaching after the first massacre. Then ten years passed until Atsiz's second massacre, so if that was a trigger, surely there would be a call to arms a few months later. No? How about a year later? No? A decade? No, it was twenty-two years and three popes later. News may have travelled slowly in medieval Europe, but not that slowly.

What was a more likely trigger occurred in early 1095 when envoys from the Byzantine Emperor Alexios Komnenos arrived to speak to Urban. The Byzantines were in desperate need of Western assistance against the relentless advances of the Turkish hordes. Alp Arslan might be dead and the Seljuk Empire might be fragmenting, but all of central Anatolia had fallen, and Alexios just didn't have the resources to win it back. But if the Pope could create an army of the famous heavy cavalry of Europe, then the Byzantines would have a suitable weapon to retaliate. In return, the Pope would get more say in the affairs of the Church in the East (the Eastern and Western Churches had split after the great schism of

1054; and while this is still the case today, more than 950 years later, at the time it looked like this call for help could patch things up).

It seems that these more worldly considerations of increased influence and power were the triggers for the speech at Claremont – and not the massacre of Christians a generation earlier.

On 27 November 1095, Pope Urban II stood in a field and preached the idea of an armed pilgrimage (technically an oxymoron), and while his exact words have been lost forever, Fulcher of Chartres recorded the highlights:

> ... Your brethren who live in the east are in urgent need of your help ... For, as the most of you have heard, the Turks and Arabs have attacked them and have conquered the territory of Romania ... They have occupied more and more of the lands of those Christians, and have overcome them in seven battles. They have killed and captured many, and have destroyed the churches and devastated the empire. If you permit them to continue thus for awhile with impunity, the faithful of God will be much more widely attacked by them.
>
> On this account I, or rather the Lord, beseech you as Christ's heralds to publish this everywhere and to persuade all people of whatever rank, foot-soldiers and knights, poor and rich, to carry aid promptly to those Christians and to destroy that vile race from the lands of our friends.

Robert the Monk adds that the Pope promised a remission of sins to all who went on this campaign. This meant that their souls would be guaranteed a place in heaven. At the end of the speech, Urban commanded *Deus Vult* (God wills it)! This turned into an ecstatic chant from the crowd and would continue to be a rallying cry in the coming march on Jerusalem.

Pope Urban II had masterfully tapped into the hopes

and fears of almost everyone in Europe. Much has been made of the motivations of the crusaders, so it's worth remembering that, like everything in life, ideas change over time. For the First Crusade (it was never referred to as that by contemporaries), there can be no doubt of the religious fervour that drove these men to march from places like the Rhineland all the way to Jerusalem.

From the point of view of any of the martial classes in Europe, this was a chance to do what they did best: fight. The only problem was that, previously, they had been constantly warned that violence would lead them to Hell and eternal damnation. Now they could fight and receive a guaranteed place in Heaven – live or die, it was a no-lose situation. We now call these men 'crusaders', but contemporary accounts of the Crusades invariably call them 'pilgrims'.

A few of these knights and aristocrats (no monarchs journeyed on the First Crusade) would become fabulously wealthy; and some may have been motivated, in a small way, by the prospect of finding booty in exotic faraway lands. The journey would be expensive, alarmingly so. To give you an idea, Robert, Duke of Normandy, put the entirety of Normandy up as a guarantee for his brother William II, King of England (both sons of William the Conqueror), to pay for him and his knights to make this journey. Putting it simply, there were easier ways to get rich than to slog your way across a continent into completely unknown lands against an unknown enemy. Far more of these knights were to die bankrupt than would win a city, county or crown.

Finally, there's Jerusalem. Rome might be the eternal city, but Jerusalem was the holy one. On almost all medieval maps of the world, Jerusalem was at the centre. It was the place where Jesus had worked, where miracles had happened; it was 'Heaven on Earth'. A chance to visit this most sacred of cities was what every Christian soul desired, and now the pope was telling them there was a divine mandate to do so. The call to Jerusalem was irresistible.

To say that the speech at Claremont created a spiritual revival is overstating things, but it was a message that everyone wanted to hear. Jerusalem was under threat from heathens, and Europe was needed to help in the fight against these infidels. It was time to go to the aid of their Orthodox cousins in the East and reclaim the holy city. All this was wrapped up with the guaranteed big bonus of safe passage to heavenly paradise. What's not to like?

But this was one speech, in one field. How did the news spread? It wasn't just from the crowd (although those who were present invariably returned to their respective homes and spread the word). The Pope had a ready-made network to publicise his views. From this point on, every pulpit in Europe preached a march on Jerusalem. The deadline for heading east was August; and across Europe, tens of thousands rallied to the cause, immensely bolstering Urban's credentials as a temporal ruler, not just a religious one. Most kings would be envious of the force that Urban's speech rallied, and even more jealous of what that army achieved.

The events of 1096, however, didn't pan out the way that either Alexios or Urban had planned. To begin with, the poor and non-aristocratic members of society wanted to do their bit too, and this resulted in completely unnecessary bloodshed.

If you were too poor to get to the Middle East, were there any nearby infidels who threatened Christendom? The logic was horribly twisted, but the conclusion was that peasants would be doing everyone a favour by attacking Jewish communities. Hadn't they killed Jesus? Actually, no, that was the Romans. Didn't they deny the divinity of Jesus? Okay, that much was true. Didn't they sacrifice Christian children? Absolutely not! But sadly, that was a general suspicion at the time.

Therefore, if you couldn't get to Jerusalem, you could always attack your local population of Jews. These shocking and pointless pogroms resulted in thousands of deaths, mainly in Germany; but they occurred against Jewish populations throughout Europe.

Sadly, this was to set a precedent; as Urban had raised the xenophobia of European Christians even higher, now any 'otherness' could be life-threatening. Time and again, then and in the years to come, a call to crusade would lead to rioting and the murder of Europe's Jewish populations.

This anti-Semitism was one unforeseen consequence of Claremont. The second was the often overlooked People's Crusade. Peter the Hermit had heard Urban's calls, and he preached zealously in France. What he created was a huge host of the poor. Society's underprivileged, including many women, flocked to him. These people knew that they would not be allowed to fight in any military campaigns, but they still felt the Lord's will in them and nursed a desire to go on pilgrimage to the Holy Land. It helped that Peter had a scroll given to him from the angels of Heaven confirming his right to lead this People's Crusade; and anyone who couldn't see the scroll was an unbeliever (a genius variation of 'the emperor's new clothes').

Peter led this rag-tag horde across Europe to Constantinople. On the way he lost thousands to bandits, desertions, illness and local attacks. However, he still had thousands with him when he arrived at the Byzantine capital city. The Byzantine Emperor Alexios was horrified. From his perspective, thousands of beggars had just turned up on his doorstep. While they were of no use to him militarily, they all needed to be fed. He quickly acquired the boats needed to get Peter and his grubby flock across to Anatolia and sent them on their way as fast as he could.

We must now think about things from the Muslim point of view. Since the death of Alp Arslan, the Seljuk Empire had disintegrated; and as the caliphate to the south had also fallen apart, these once-great empires were reduced to warring principalities. The 1090s were a time of chaos in the Middle East. There was a power vacuum, and as we all know, nature abhors a vacuum. Urban's speech had gone completely unnoticed by Muslim potentates. While in general the West has specific sources for each crusade, the Islamic chronicles are not so easily sorted.

The news of a great host heading into Anatolia caused consternation. Was this a fresh Byzantine offensive or something completely new? The Turks were the first to probe the defences of this travelling rabble. It was too large to be pilgrims, yet too poorly equipped to be an army. The Turks became bolder in their attacks, and what happened to the People's Crusade is what happens to an ice cube in water. It grew smaller and smaller until there was nothing left. There was no pivotal battle and no epic last stand. What chance did a bunch of beggars, civilians and women have against some of the finest horsemen in the medieval world?

Those who weren't killed were captured and sold into slavery. A few managed to avoid either of those fates and somehow managed to get back to Constantinople. These included Peter; it seems God had given him a second chance to carry out his divine wishes, or else he was the kind of guy who knew how to save his own skin. Either way, he still had a further part to play in the story of the First Crusade.

But Peter probably did the main military crusade a favour. The Turks were slower to respond to the second incursion than the first, and this could well have been because they thought the second body of Europeans were the same as the first. They couldn't have been more mistaken.

From the winter of 1096 to the spring of 1097, the princes of Europe arrived in Constantinople, with thousands of heavy cavalry, archers, crossbowmen, sappers, spearmen and infantry. This was more like it – and exactly what Alexios had been hoping for. However, before he could allow such a potentially dangerous host of armed men into his capital, he needed their leaders to swear oaths of allegiance. This was a wise precaution from his point of view, but created an existential quandary for the European nobility.

As part of a feudal system, a noble (a baron, count, duke, etc.) would have to swear an oath of loyalty to his master and provide men for his lord's army. In return he could run his lands pretty much as he liked. At the top of this pyramid of power stood the king; each layer underneath owed allegiance to the immediate lord above it. Alexios was asking for his own oath. What if the two oaths created contradictions?

While all this was happening, there was political and military manoeuvring. The arrival of each new European detachment meant more mouths to feed, but also a more potent weapon for Alexios to wield. However, there were skirmishes between the crusaders and the Byzantine forces, even minor sieges and the mutual holding of hostages. Things were tense.

One of the first to arrive was Hugh of Vermandois (and who was there in Constantinople, waiting for the main crusade to turn up? None other than Peter the Hermit). Slowly, over the weeks, Alexios restricted Hugh's movements until he became a virtual prisoner. After this event, the more high-profile arrival of Godfrey de Bouillon led to a brief siege of an imperial palace and, ultimately, to an agreement on a compromise oath. Others, such as Bohemund of Taranto (Italian by birth but of Norman stock), swore the oath more easily, but he had been in open war against Byzantine lands only recently. How seriously did he take this agreement?

By spring of 1097, with Byzantine support, the European

crusaders headed into Anatolia. The agreement with Alexios was simple: he would aid them when he could, but they must return all the lands in Anatolia to him, up to and including the key city of Antioch in the south-east of Asia Minor. We know a lot about Alexios from his remarkable daughter, Anna Komnene, who wrote an entire biography of her father, making her a rare female writer in this age. She portrays her father as powerful but also as a careful negotiator, something worth remembering.

The Crusades are often seen as Christianity versus Islam, and, as we will see later, this became a gross simplification; but from the outset, in the Middle East at least, there were three distinct groups at play. The Muslims were not a united front, and this helped the crusaders since they did not face the coordinated efforts of an Asian empire, which surely would have annihilated them before they got anywhere near Jerusalem. Next, there were the knights from Europe, who were always strangers in a strange land. And then there were the Byzantines, who had their own agenda. They used the crusaders' religious zeal to patch up their old empire, to push back the decades of Turkish successes and to breathe new life into an ancient empire.

This time the plan worked and both the crusaders and the Byzantines, while at times edgy and distrustful of each other, worked effectively enough to achieve an apparently miraculous victory. In this situation both the Byzantines and the Europeans were happy. However, it wouldn't always be that way.

Just two months later, the crusade had arrived at Nicaea, a key Byzantine city that had fallen to the Turks some fifteen years earlier. It sat on a lake and had become the capital city of the Sultanate of Rum, a fragment of the old Seljuk Empire. It was usually home to Kilij Arslan. Kilij, despite his surname, was not a son of Alp (Arslan, or sometimes Aslan, is Turkic for lion. Where do you think

C. S. Lewis got the name from?). He had even been held captive by Alp Arslan's son for a while. However, Kilij was the epitome of Turkish martial prowess and needless violence. This was a man who had carved out a powerful dominion from nothing, who had murdered his father-in-law and who had been instrumental in the eradication of the People's Crusade. He was a cold, calculating killer – and Nicaea was his prized jewel.

However, thinking this crusade was the same deal as the People's Crusade, he had left only a lone garrison at the city, along with his family and entire treasury. They would be safe from a rabble, but not from the cream of Europe's fighting men. The crusaders were to make their very first enemy.

The crusaders tried surrounding the city, but with a lake on one side this was impossible. However, some of the Turkish garrison sallied forth from a gate and engaged in the first proper battle of the medieval Crusades. The Turks were hopelessly outnumbered, so after a brief skirmish most retreated; however, a few had other orders and broke free from the engagement to ride out to the east to warn Kilij of the danger his capital faced. He arrived a few days later and the ensuing battle became a monumental cavalry engagement. While Kilij had underestimated the size of the crusader force, he fought long into the night trying to break the Franks and get to his capital. Eventually, and after a long and bloody battle, he was beaten back. The warlord knew a no-win situation when he saw one and retreated, presumably swearing revenge.

For the siege to work, the crusaders needed to block off the lake to ensure complete envelopment of the city. At this point Alexios arrived with his army and ordered a number of boats to be dragged across land and into Lake Ascanius.

From the defenders' point of view, this was game over. With their leader beaten back and the city now surrounded, it was better to negotiate peace than to allow an assault and a bloody sacking. However, rather than discussing it with Bohemund and his cohorts, Alexios got in early and sorted the whole thing out, much to the consternation of the crusaders. It was even done with a fake assault of the walls to make the Byzantines appear to have captured it in battle.

Once in, there was little bloodshed, as Alexios wisely ensured that the crusaders could not come in more than ten at a time. He replenished their supplies and horses, and the crusade left in high spirits after a relatively easy victory. On reflection, hadn't they promised to obey Alexios and return all the spoils of war before Antioch?

The crusade carried on further into the Anatolian hinterland. As others had earlier learned, June and July in that region are like a furnace. The temperatures regularly go above 40° Celsius, and streams, rivers or even shelter are hard to find. By now Bohemund had become the de facto leader of the European crusaders and had split the force to allow an easier time of provisioning in such a sparse area. As they were now deep in enemy territory this was a risky strategy, but there was no other realistic option. As soon as they left Nicaea in their various divisions, it became obvious that they were being shadowed by a Turkish force.

Kilij Arslan had regrouped and created an alliance with the Danishmends' Emir (while this looks like 'Danish Men', they were actually another group of Turks who would normally have fought against Kilij but had recognised that it was in their interests to destroy this crusader army). On 1 July the Turks' occasional skirmishes and hit-and-run attacks turned into a full-blown battle. The Battle of Dorylaeum was so called because it happened near(ish) the ruins of this ancient city. It should really have been called the battle in the middle of nowhere. Kilij had chosen his spot well, and as the crusader troops were now travelling in small clumps it was the perfect place to attack the vanguard under Bohemund.

Bohemund ordered all the non-combatants to create a defensive camp and led the knights out to fight. This was the first time the Christian heavy cavalry was pitted against the light Turkish horse archers. The heavy cavalry should have crushed them, but if the Turks had room to manoeuvre then the knights could never make their superior arms and armour count. It was like a bull facing a matador. The Turks excelled at riding up close, firing arrows from their composite bows (which had similar draw power to a longbow) and hitting their target while at a full gallop. European mail armour was of only limited use against the piercing nature of arrows; and while their large shields and padded undershirts would have helped, some of the knights must have looked like hedgehogs by the end of the battle – the ones that were still alive.

Kilij threw everything he had at these invaders. His family members were now Byzantine captives, and as his reputation rested on martial prowess the loss of his capital could be his undoing – unless he inflicted a crushing defeat here and now. In all the confusion, Bohemund and his knights were thrown back to the defended camp and surrounded.

As the horse archers ground down the crusaders, the battle looked like turning into a massacre; but just as the camp's defences began to buckle, Godfrey of Bouillon and Raymond of Toulouse arrived with their contingents and forced the Turks to break off their encirclement. As the day progressed, every time the Turks reinstated their dominance on the field, a new section of the crusader army arrived just in the nick of time.

One of these was led by Bishop Adhemar of Le Puy, who arrived late in the day. He had been sent as Papal Legate (representative) on the expedition, but he was a hands-on military man when needed. In this situation he led troops into the Turkish camp and ordered it to be set on fire. After a day of being thwarted by continual reinforcements, seeing their camp on fire was the last straw for the Turks. They broke off and retreated. The crusade survived, but it had been a close-run thing. That they had been lucky was acknowledged by all involved, but why had they had good luck? This narrow escape was turned into a sign of divine blessing, that Jesus and the saints were watching over them and ensuring victory (although surely if God had really been protecting them, he wouldn't have allowed the ambush in the first place). Regardless of the narrowness of the victory, Dorylaeum had been another victory and a further boost to the morale of the Christians.

The Turks had thrown everything they had at this army and failed. While raids continued, there were no more pitched battles as the crusaders marched through central Anatolia. Kilij Arslan had left them a farewell gift: he had burned and destroyed as much as he could to ensure the crusaders got as little sustenance as possible. This march would be remembered more bitterly than the earlier battles. Men started dying of thirst; the horses were dying too, while some knights were reduced to riding cows. Had the Muslims formed a coalition and attacked them again, it was likely that the crusade would crumble, but their two previous decisive victories stopped any of the local emirs from doing anything too rash.

Just as Russia grinds down armies with distance and cold, Anatolia was doing the same with distance and heat. Chronicles describe mothers leaving their babies on the sides of the path. Raymond of Toulouse fell so ill that he was read his last rites, although he did recover.

While this was terrible for all involved, it does seem that the crusaders had deliberately chosen this route. They were avoiding the northern Muslim princes whose power bases had not yet been touched; and the crusade as a whole was heading towards the Cilician Gates, a gap in the mountains that would lead them into a less hostile area. The crusaders must have had guides, maps or local assistance, because the path they took, while arduous, was also the smartest, even though the army had to split up into smaller groups to get to key locations on the way to their next target at Antioch. But the unrelenting heat and desolate landscape made the summer of 1097 one of the lowest points of the whole campaign.

Meanwhile, Baldwin of Boulogne set off even further east to the Armenian area of Edessa (this is now roughly the area where Iran, Iraq and Turkey meet). Here he met Thoros, the regional lord, and in a matter of months had sweet-talked his way into becoming his adopted son and heir. The timing for Baldwin was excellent because in March 1098, while the rest of the crusade was still at Antioch, Thoros was assassinated (it's possible Baldwin may have had a hand in this, but Thoros had many enemies), and Baldwin became the Count of Edessa. This was the very first Crusader State, a new power base which allowed Baldwin both to attack nearby Muslim potentates and send supplies to the ongoing siege at Antioch.

The crusaders' arrival into Armenian Christian Cilicia meant a safe haven, allowing the Christians time to regroup and focus on their task ahead. Antioch was one of the great cities of the Near East; it was also one of the first cities to have a Christian community and had been a seat of one of the patriarchs for centuries. It was enormous, larger than any in western Europe at the time, and was defended by a massive wall bristling with towers. This was the final prize that Alexios had required as part of his oath and, as such, an important city. It was obvious why he'd want it back.

The Christians didn't have nearly enough troops to

surround the city, but it had fallen to treachery before. All that was needed was someone to open a gate in the dead of night, and it would be easy to infiltrate it. However, nobody inside seemed willing to oblige and the siege of Antioch was to go down in history as one of the most epic.

It was a hideous stalemate. The crusade was too small to get in, and the garrison of Antioch too small to defeat the Christians in battle, so the siege dragged on. The crusaders arrived in October 1097, just as the weather was starting to cool, which meant that many of the nearby crops had already been brought into the city. There was never a better time to bolt the gates and hope for a relief army.

In December, as provisions became harder to come by, the crusaders were forced to scavenge further and further afield in order to get food back to the camps. It was during one of these foraging missions that Bohemund and Robert of Flanders discovered a relief army, led by Duqaq of Aleppo. Duqaq and Rudwan of Damascus were brothers and had been fighting a civil war over the ownership of Syria when this strange western army arrived from Anatolia. Antioch was a great prize, and anyone who could save it from the Christians would have the upper hand. Duqaq got there first, but the accidental discovery of his army before it had had a chance to reach the crusader camp was a disaster for him. This time the crusaders had the advantage of surprise and Duqaq was thoroughly routed.

This engagement showed the dangers of spreading the crusading army too thin in hostile territory. How long could their luck hold? Rudwan arrived later and met the same fate as his brother. This was the third Turkish ruler of considerable local stature to face a humiliating defeat at the hands of these strangers. Were they blessed by God? For the time being the crusade was safe – as safe as you can be besieging a mighty fortified city.

Foraging parties, Byzantine food supplies, the occasional

wagon train from Edessa; these were all essential lifelines for a dwindling effort. As 1097 turned into 1098, food stocks were dangerously low. It was noted that Peter the Hermit had travelled this far, but was caught attempting to slink off, presumably thinking this crusade was in danger of becoming like the one he had led.

Disease broke out and there was cannibalism. Why let an enemy corpse rot when it could give life? Disease-ridden cannibals, intent on breaking into a mighty city, itching to have their revenge on the population, had nothing to do with Jesus' teachings. This is what these Christian soldiers, allegedly fighting for God, had descended into.

The remaining Byzantine soldiers left with their general, and the weeks dragged on with no sign of capitulation on either side. Life in Antioch was also becoming grim. Their own food stores were running low, and the barbaric corpse-eating army outside its gates refused to leave.

In March 1098 there was some relief when a crusader fleet arrived with fresh troops and food, but all it seemed to do was prolong the agony. It wasn't enough to tip the balance in favour of the crusade. Then, in May, terrible news: Kerbogha, another fearsome Turkish warlord, had forged several alliances and could arrive at any time. This was a very dangerous situation. The Christian army was physically weak; it could either stand and fight and face total annihilation, or leave Antioch after all these months, with nothing to show for it.

Bohemund saved the day, but his price would be heavy. Firstly, he openly demanded the official leadership of the crusade (Adhemar had always been the spiritual leader and remained so). The other nobles agreed. Secondly, he got them to agree that he should have Antioch, and not Alexios. This was easier to agree since all the Greek generals had left, and Alexios had not gone through the privations that everyone else, including Bohemund, had endured. He then revealed he had been in talks with a man called Firouz, who was willing to betray the city.

There are several stories to explain why Firouz would do this, but for me the most convincing was that he had been discovered hoarding food, a crime punishable by death during a siege. So to save his own skin, make a lot of money and, of course, stay on the winning side, he promised to open a gate on 3 June, eight months after the arrival of the crusade at Antioch.

That night Bohemund ordered the army to march away from the walls to lower suspicions. (It was at this point that Stephen of Blois permanently left the crusade.) Then, under the cover of darkness, the army returned and Firouz, true to his word, let them in. The Christians quickly set upon the governor and all the civilians they could lay they hands on. Thousands were slain, including Firouz's own brother. This was how the Western Christians behaved on their first occupation of a Muslim city. To be fair, after eight months the occupants could expect little mercy, but it was still savagery.

On 4 June, the crusaders realised that the garrison remained in its citadel, too strong to be attacked by them in their weakened state. Then, on the 5th, Kerbogha arrived with his army, two days late. He had tried, on the way, to conquer Baldwin in Edessa and had spent three weeks in the effort, to no avail. Knowing he had to move on, he finally did so, but the distraction at Edessa resulted in his arriving just a little too late to catch the crusaders outside the walls. Did this matter? True, the crusaders were now behind the walls, but the city was empty of food. All that had happened was role reversal, with the Christians now the besieged, rather than the besiegers. They were still weak and disease-ridden, but now they were facing a large, fresh army led by a veteran general.

The initial victory had been very temporary. Morale

collapsed, desertions rose; it seemed that Kerbogha might not need to fight to beat the crusaders. The next event can be seen either as a miracle or a bit of theatrical hustling. Peter Bartholomew (not Peter the Hermit) had visions from Saint Andrew telling him where the Holy Lance (the spear that pierced Jesus' side during the crucifixion, hugely popular with knights as it symbolised both Jesus and war) had been buried in Antioch. He started excavating the church of Saint Peter, and on 14 June a piece of iron was revealed, one which Peter confirmed was the Holy Lance. It was a miracle and a divine sign that God would let the crusade triumph over these insurmountable odds.

Adhemar of Le Puy, the official Papal Legate, was less than convinced by all this. But Bohemund desperately needed a break, so he enthusiastically paraded the 'lance' around the troops. The results were electrifying. Now they could all see tangible evidence that Jesus and the saints were with them. They could fight and win. But as so often in history, things weren't quite that neat. Before any rash battles, Bohemund sent out Peter the Hermit, who had been delivering some inspiring sermons after the fall of Antioch, to see if he could negotiate with the Muslims. He came back empty-handed, but the mission was a sign that he had secured a new position of power within the crusade's council. More importantly, Bohemund would have happily negotiated his way out of the situation rather than trust only in God.

On 28 June, the crusade took a huge gamble. It came out of the gates of Antioch, right in front of Kerbogha's army, and formed up to do battle. Had the Muslims attacked as the crusade reformed its ranks, victory would have been assured. But from the Muslim point of view, things weren't that simple. As already stated, there was no central authority; and the Fatimid (Egyptian) Muslim contingent of Kerbogha's coalition left as soon as the Christians formed ranks, not because they were cowards but because victory would have made Kerbogha even more powerful than he was already. The Fatimids were far more worried about him than about any threat from the Christians. It's a reminder that no side was completely united; and while it's natural to split things according to religious motivations, sometimes more earthly priorities got in the way.

Duqaq was also present at the battle, looking for revenge, but to have fought under his enemies' banners would have been deeply uncomfortable for him. So, from the Islamic point of view, the Christians were allowed to form up in battle readiness because of dynastic bickering. It was an army waiting to shatter. But the Christians knew none of this at this time, so they explained it on a spiritual level. First-hand accounts, like the *Gesta Francorum*, make references to visions and images of the saints themselves, right there at the battle. Saint George (chosen because of his association with martial prowess) was seen to be fighting side by side with the flesh and blood men of the crusade. Unbelievably, and against all the odds, the Muslims broke and fled. They left behind them their entire camp. The concubines and servants were slaughtered, while the food, riches and tents provided welcome relief for this army on the brink of collapse. The exhausted, starving and sick Christians had vanquished what seemed an unstoppable foe. *Deus Vult*, indeed!

So once again the Christian forces appeared to have divine blessing. From the point of view of the Muslims, this filthy rabble seemed unstoppable; every time success seemed assured, defeat was snatched from the jaws of victory. For the time being, the Muslim princes left this strange, invincible army alone.

What next in Antioch? After such a gruelling siege, it was wise to take stock. The crusade had lost momentum badly; it had been at the same location for about a year. Recuperation revived rivalries, and the less than holy squabbling began. The main split was between the southern and northern Europeans, but the competitive rivalry that had pushed them against seemingly overwhelming odds now threatened to engulf the expedition as a whole.

Plague broke out, and it didn't help that the man who could have been seen as a neutral arbitrator, Adhemar, died in August 1098 from the sickness sweeping through Antioch. The political wrangling continued into 1099, when – finally – most of the force continued on its way to Jerusalem. Bohemund had captured the prize and became Prince of Antioch. This was to be an explicit breaking of the oath with Alexios; but in reality, he was too far away to do anything other than send threatening letters via embassies.

So the rump of the force that had originally left Byzantine lands continued to march south. What had been a force of 30,000–40,000 was now little more than 10,000 strong. However, the reputation of these barbarians was such that all the local Muslim potentates would rather sign peace treaties and resupply them than fight them. There was an aborted siege at Arqa, a Fatimid and Muslim stronghold. The Fatimid authorities made a peace deal on the condition that the crusade did not march on Jerusalem, but this was ignored.

On arrival at Tripoli the crusade was welcomed by its lord, who was an enemy of the Fatimids. He was another Muslim who resupplied them, and according to the *Gesta Francorum* promised to convert to Christianity (this never happened). The march from Antioch to Jerusalem is a further example of the myth that the Crusades were a clash of civilisations. The Muslim princes of the Middle East had plenty of time to raise another force if the real fear was a Christian army in Muslim lands. Instead, we see that political realities always took precedence; and had it not been for the power vacuum, and the hospitality of some of these local governors, the crusade would probably have never got within viewing distance of Jerusalem.

On 6 June 1099, Godfrey and Bohemund's nephew, Tancred, reached Bethlehem, where he planted his banner on the Church of the Nativity. It had taken three years, but this was what the crusaders had come for. Now they were in the lands that Jesus himself had known; they were walking among the stories from the Bible. The next day they arrived at their ultimate destination, Jerusalem. While it truly must have been a great sight for sore eyes, it didn't fundamentally alter the now obvious divisions in the crusading forces.

Jerusalem has had more than its fair share of sieges, but what the crusaders didn't know was that the city had changed hands only a year before. For a generation it had been under Seljuk Turkish rule, but as that empire crumbled, the Fatimids in the south had taken advantage of the situation and captured the city in 1098. The siege on that occasion was nothing spectacular, and, from the point of view of the average denizen of Jerusalem, nothing much changed.

The new governor of Jerusalem, Iftikhar ad-Dawla, had known the Christians were coming. He prepared as best he could. The Christian community was expelled (probably quite rightly) as he feared betrayal from that section of the population. He also poisoned the wells outside the city walls.

Godfrey and Tancred set up camp north of the city; Raymond of Toulouse set up to the west. This was less tactical and more to do with the internal rivalries of the expedition. Even in the face of their ultimate goal, the crusade was divided by petty arguments. There was an initial assault on 13 June, which some lords did not join, not because of cowardice but, again, because of politics. Just as we have witnessed with the Muslim lords, the political agendas in the Christian camp frequently trumped spiritual ones. All of these men had marched across Europe and Asia Minor for a spiritual imperative, but they now squabbled before the holy city; the irony was lost on them.

The initial assault, which was repelled, was really a chance to probe the defences. It was vital to do so because there was now news of a Fatimid relief army marching from Egypt. It's at this point that Adhemar appears again in the story, which is odd, as he'd been dead for nearly a year. The Papal Legate had been hugely popular with the average soldier on this armed pilgrimage, so once again, the believable is intertwined with the mystical. There are accounts of visions of Adhemar telling the crusaders to fast for three days and then march in barefoot procession around the walls of Jerusalem. If they did this, Jerusalem would fall in nine days, following the Biblical example of Joshua at the siege of Jericho.

Again there is a blurring of what to modern eyes looks like historical fact and religious myth. It is an example of how the mysterious and the normal swirled in the minds of our medieval ancestors. This story was not just made up for cynical manipulation; people believed, just as they believed that successfully assaulting Jerusalem was God's will and that this would ensure them an eternity in heaven.

The procession was carried out to the general bemusement of the onlooking Muslim garrison in the city. The barefoot march culminated on the Mount of Olives, where Peter the Hermit (who always seemed to know the right thing to say) preached to the penitents in front of him. By now the crusaders knew that a relief Fatimid army was on its way, so the combination of worldly practicalities and spiritual motivation led to a rapprochement between the various crusader factions still jostling for power. They had to storm Jerusalem or face annihilation; the arguing could wait.

The crusaders attacked from both the north and the south on 13 July. In the baking heat they climbed siege ladders and fought on battlements, drenched in sweat under their heavy European armour. The force in the south was reaching deadlock, but Godfrey and Tancred were starting to make some headway in the north.

For the Christians, there was no option. They were exhausted; there was no time for a long siege, particularly with a fresh army on its way – Palestine in high summer meant there was little chance of getting an extensive resupply. It was now or never.

On 15 July, in a last desperate push, the inner rampart of the northern wall was captured by Godfrey and Tancred. Now the garrison of the city was stretched. Should it bolster the defence in the north and risk weakening its solid defence of the southern gates? During this decision-making pause, with panic spreading through the Muslim troops, the defenders abandoned the walls. The crusaders lost no time, and tenuous breaches turned into a full-scale rush into the city. Jerusalem had fallen. Or, as the Christians saw it, the city tainted with alien religions had been freed.

The relief, the religious fervour, the anxiety of four years manifested itself in a shameful culmination. The crusaders attacked and massacred as much of the population as they could get their hands on.

Some historians have pointed out that the Christian sources of the massacre are apocalyptic and feel like scenes from the Book of Revelation. Here's the *Gesta Francorum* (written by an anonymous knight from the Crusade, so an eyewitness account):

> The pilgrims chased the saracens, killing them as they went, so that their blood flowed all over the Temple ... in the morning our men climbed onto the roof of the Temple and

> attacked the saracens both male and female, and behead
> them with unsheathed swords ... The other saracens threw
> themselves from the temple ... such a slaughter of pagans no
> one has ever seen or heard of.

The argument is that, to make the event more biblical, the extent of the massacre was exaggerated; horses wading up to their bridles in blood (described in another source) is simply impossible. However, the massacre did happen, and it was appalling. The temple mentioned above was the Temple Mount, site of the Dome of the Rock, where Tancred massacred a host of Muslim civilians before ordering a halt. Events that justifiably appalled and disgusted Muslim historians (far more than the sacking of Antioch) were backed up by Christian chronicles and don't bear too much critical analysis. There is no way to diminish what was terrible bloodshed, let alone bloodshed inflicted on a population that had endured a siege just a year before. Muslims, Jews and even some Christians were murdered with fire or steel; thousands, if not tens of thousands, were butchered. It was not the first bloody end to a siege of Jerusalem, but it was the first in over 1,000 years (the last one had been Titus at the head of a Roman army).

This was terrifying to the Islamic Middle East. This strange army had exploded from the west, torn its way across Asia Minor and Syria, had seemingly been on the brink of defeat numerous times, only to crush everything the Muslim world could throw at it – and now this band of barbarians had captured Jerusalem (called Al-Quds in Arabic, meaning 'the Holy') and treated this holy city in the most shocking way.

Iftikhar al-Dawla, the military commander, did a deal with Raymond, surrendering the citadel in return for safe passage out of the charnel house. The crusaders let him go and continued their bloody rampage. In the face of such savagery, who can blame Iftikhar al-Dawla for leaving while he could? Many prisoners who had surrendered during the frenzy of killing were later executed, showing a veritable compulsion by the Christians to exterminate the occupants of the city.

A few days later, with bloated bodies rotting where they had fallen, flies swarming and streets caked with black blood, the crusade held a religious service. This was followed by a council in the Church of the Holy Sepulchre to create a king for the newly created Kingdom of Jerusalem. Raymond of Toulouse was first choice but refused in a show of piety, probably hoping that his humility would lead to him being crowned. However, if this was his plan it backfired spectacularly, as Godfrey was then nominated, and unlike Raymond he didn't hesitate. Even so, Godfrey used the ambiguous term *princeps* rather than *rex* ('king' in Latin). Afterwards, Raymond took his men and flounced out of the city in a great big sulk.

Godfrey barely had time to choose a palace because now he had a kingdom to defend, and a Fatimid army was getting ever closer. The Fatimids, led by vizier al-Afdal Shahanshah, had a polyglot army of about 40,000. The vizier commanded Turks, Arabs, Persians, Kurds and even Christian Armenians. So Godfrey scraped together a force of just over 10,000 and marched south.

Crucially, the crusaders discovered the massive Fatimid army (about four times the size of the Christian forces) first and did the only thing they could do: attack and hope that surprise and God's will would be enough to prevail. The Battle of Ascalon is often seen as the end of the First Crusade, but it wasn't (more on this later). Under Godfrey, Tancred and Robert of Normandy (son of William the Conqueror), the European heavy cavalry shattered the completely unprepared Fatimid army. Al-Afdal Shahanshah fled to the nearby citadel of Ascalon (hence the name of the battle) and the next day retreated from these fortifications with the rump of his force. The crusaders fell on the rich camp and supplies. Victory was complete. The crusaders were here to stay.

3

A New Type of Crusade: The Second Crusade and the Rise of Saladin

Pope Urban II never did get to hear of the fall of Jerusalem because he died in 1099. However, the new Pope, Paschal II, was ecstatic with the news. Without a doubt, the whole endeavour fundamentally changed forever the psyche of European society. This fervour for continued Christian success did not launch the Second Crusade (that was to come a generation later), but instead rallied the soldiers who had taken the crusaders' vows but had not gone on crusade.

This included Stephen of Blois, who by now was a pariah in Europe, having deserted the expedition just before the victory at Antioch. It was said that his wife was so disgusted with his conduct that she refused to sleep with him (and most men have been forced to sleep on the couch for less).

Between 1100 and 1101, at least three major armies marched into Anatolia hoping to recreate the success of their fellow Christian knights. While a few of these soldiers did make it to the Holy Land as much-needed replacements, these expeditions were nowhere near as successful. Up until 1100 the Muslims had concluded that the crusaders were invincible and that whole new strategies would be needed to defeat them; but almost as soon as this sheen of invulnerability appeared, it faded as these other (mainly

Germanic) expeditions perished in exactly the way the First Crusade should have.

Kilij Arslan had lost vital prestige because of his setbacks against the First Crusade. He could not survive more failures. The battles of Mersivan and Heraclea may have happened at different times, in different parts of Anatolia, but they were essentially a rerun of Dorylaeum – except now the crusaders ran out of luck. Kilij had allied himself with Rudwan of Aleppo and showed these Christian forces what Muslim armies could do when unified. Harassing the slow-moving European forces with horse archers and choosing the site of battle to allow his lighter cavalry room for manoeuvre against the heavy armour of the knights gave Kilij the victories he so badly needed.

These new crusading armies, who brought desperately needed fresh troops to the Holy Land, were crushed. Just a year after the fall of Jerusalem, Islam was in the ascendency once more. These battles have been largely forgotten by everyone. Muslim historians don't tend to mention them because, in the short term, they didn't change the status quo. After all, this was the start of the crusading movement in the Middle East, not the end. As for the European chroniclers, they were hardly going to spend too much time tainting the achievements of the so-called First Crusade by adding such a depressing sequel.

However, these forgotten crusading armies shed important light on just how lucky Bohemund and his company had been. Had Urban preached ten years earlier or later than he did, the crusade would have run into a relatively unified Muslim Middle East. It was complete chance that this armed pilgrimage stumbled through an area that was struggling to come to terms with dramatic shifts in power between the local warlords.

Marching across Anatolia in summer nearly undid the First Crusade, not just at the Battle of Dorylaeum but in the desperate march to escape enemy territory afterwards. Jerusalem was a very long way away from Europe, and the only way to get there was either by treacherous sea routes or a march over hundreds of miles of scorching desert, constantly harassed by Muslim horse archers. Crusading was expensive, dangerous and very time-consuming.

It was this serendipity (from the Christian point of view), this blind luck and tenacity, that had suddenly created from out of nowhere a Christian sphere of influence in the Middle East, and these Westerners were putting down roots. There was now the County of Edessa (the most northern and eastern state), the Principality of Antioch (land based around the city), the County of Tripoli (linking the area of Antioch to the lower, key kingdom) and the Kingdom of Jerusalem.

However, these Crusader States were not the only Christian encroachment into a Muslim sphere of influence. When Urban urged the cream of European knights to march east, he deliberately left out the Christian forces of Spain. He specified that they continue their own war against the infidel closer to home. Urban wanted control of what were presumed to be Christian lands in the Iberian Peninsula.

The gradual conquest of Muslim territory in modern-day Spain and Portugal has become known as the *Reconquista*. It was no such thing. In one word, you get an image of Christian princes taking back what had once been theirs. It also implies that there was an overarching strategy. None of this is true.

The fight against the Muslim invaders of southern Europe had started with Charles Martel (see Chapter 1), but most of the Iberian Peninsula had been Muslim for centuries and relatively happily so, compared to what had been going on in the rest of Europe in the ninth century. By the time of the Council of Claremont, approximately 20 per cent of the country (mostly in the north) was ruled by Christian princes. The rest wasn't and would remain out of reach of Christian armies for centuries.

These Iberian frontier zones bore similarities to the emerging Crusader States. It was never as simple in either case as 'Muslims versus Christians'. Neither religion was unified behind one common goal. Politics always got in the way of spiritual unity. So in Spanish kingdoms like Aragon and in Palestine, Christian princes hired Muslim scholars to teach their children, alliances would be drawn up between Muslims and Christian rulers, and mercenaries of both religions could be hired by anyone with deep enough pockets.

Take for example the Kingdom of Castile. In the generation just before the First Crusade, Sancho II of Castile wanted to reunite the kingdom of his father, which had slipped into civil war. This was a case of Christians fighting Christians, as the Muslim Moors stood on the sidelines and watched. However, Sancho had an ally: Rodrigo Diaz (known to history and moviegoers as El Cid). Unfortunately Sancho died in 1072 at the siege of Zamora, which was being executed against a Christian rebel noble. El Cid may forever be remembered as a brave Christian knight fighting against the Moors, but he spent many months in the saddle suppressing insurrections against Christians, too.

Sancho's successor was King Alfonso VI, who, on paper at least, seemed to be a real crusader, conquering the Muslim Taifa kingdom of Toledo in 1085. However, on closer inspection, while battles were fought and the outcome was the same, there was no single campaign that brought him total victory. It took him decades to complete, much of it through treaties and charters with local populations or, failing that, population resettlement. On the surface it looked like a crusade, and by now the language of campaigning in Iberia was very similar to that used with regard to the Holy Land, but the reality was that wars in Spain had always been about land and power. It was coincidence that many of the vying princes happened to have different faiths.

The advantage to the Christians was that the Crusades added new impetus and interest in these wars. Are you a young knight looking to go on crusade? Too poor to go to the Holy Land but still want to fight for God against Saracens? Then come to Spain! It's closer, cheaper and you can still kill Muslims! As we will see later, even declared crusades would be influenced by the events in Iberia.

As Spain and Portugal show, what we consider to be 'Christian Europe' had yet to become fully Christian. While there were to be raids by North African Muslim pirates in southern Europe for many centuries to come, there were other areas of Europe that still resisted the Gospels. Huge areas of Eastern Europe, such as Lithuania, were still pagan. The Northern Crusades have yet to enter our story, but from the very beginning of the Crusades, God's work didn't necessarily demand that you had to go to Jerusalem. The Holy Land was the 'best' destination – the one a crusader would always aspire to – but it was by no means the only option.

After the success of the First Crusade, it became a test of manhood for every nobleman to fight in some sort of crusade. Even those of the highest birth felt obliged to take the cross (swear an oath to go on crusade). This idea of going to foreign lands to fight for a cause other than your king's was new, but fitted perfectly into the idea of chivalry, the knightly codes of honour, piety and martial prowess.

This concept of fighting for God reached a logical conclusion with the phenomenon of the military orders. In Islam a holy warrior who fights the *jihad* (which actually means 'struggle', so while it's used as the Muslim version of 'crusade', it is actually more general than that) is called a mujahideen. He is a holy warrior, fighting for Allah and remaining true to his teachings. These men weren't a special or specific unit in a Muslim army; the mujahideen were never formally organised, but a regular army might suddenly acquire that term if it fought for righteousness.

Inadvertently the West created the same thing, calling them the military orders, only the Christians went one step further. The three key orders were the Knights Hospitaller, the Poor Fellow-Soldiers of Christ and of the Temple of Solomon (I will call them the Knights Templar or the Templars – because everyone else does and it's shorter) and finally the Order of Brothers of the German House of Saint Mary in Jerusalem (again, to be more succinct, the Teutonic Knights).

These organisations (and there were many, many more, my favourite being the Knights of St Lazarus, a group of knights all afflicted with leprosy who would fight to the death) became extremely popular and enormously powerful in Europe and the Middle East. The Hospitallers were founded first in 1099, a fact that was later formally confirmed by the Pope in 1113. They were created for a number of reasons, but the key one was to help pilgrims in the Holy Land. Here they would tend to the sick in purpose-built 'hospitals' (we get the word from this military order) and also protect pilgrims from attack. Pilgrims were not allowed to carry weapons, which was why attacking them was so anathema. It also made the term 'armed pilgrims', often used by contemporaries to describe the First Crusade, sound strange.

In essence these knights were monks, residing in monasteries (albeit usually taking the form of castles) and living lives of poverty and chastity. They would spend their days either tending to the sick or, more importantly, fighting for God. These men tended to be the third or fourth sons of the aristocrats of Europe. After producing an heir and a spare, the other sons (and bastards) tended to be put into

Church positions; but for those not cut out to be bishops, here was something far more exciting. The military orders rapidly became the elite troops of Europe in the Middle East.

They also tended to be zealots (all that fighting with no female companionship can do that to men). These knights would almost always have been found where battle was hottest, giving no quarter and asking none. Their bases became the best-defended sites in the world, places where money generated from the huge endowments they steadily accrued ensured that nothing but the best materials, using the most cutting-edge theories of construction, were good enough. The end result? Crac des Chevaliers. This castle in modern-day Syria is seen, quite simply, as the best medieval castle in the world. A handful of knights could defend this fortress against a whole army. It may have been the pinnacle, but it wasn't their only mighty fortress; and while they didn't appear overnight, over decades a network of extremely formidable castles sprung up in the Holy Land, almost all paid for and manned by the military orders.

The construction lessons learned in the Middle East were brought back to Europe, and the stonemasonry of both churches and castles noticeably improved after the First Crusade. Throughout Europe, new ideas were flooding in from east to west. It wasn't just construction either. The local Christian nobles recognised the finer things the Muslims had available: silks for clothing; bath houses, which inspired a major step forwards in European hygiene; and spices, like pepper, added to food, the taste for which spread back to Christendom.

The phenomenon of the crusading movement had advantages and disadvantages for the Christian states in the Middle East. From the outset, there was the perennial problem of too few men to fight. The Christians, in somewhere like the Kingdom of Jerusalem, were an elite group of nobles who could provide the heavy cavalry, but the reality was that this minority ruled a multicultural society. Most of their subjects were Muslims, and they couldn't always be trusted to garrison fortresses, in case they decided they had more in common with the attackers than their masters.

The knights themselves weren't exactly numerous (even including the military orders), and the territory they controlled was small and agriculturally poor compared to the power bases of their enemies, like the Fatimids in Egypt. However, the regular infusions of fresh troops from Europe could help at the most opportune times. From the Muslim point of view, if one Christian army was defeated, it was often replaced with an unpredictable flow of new forces coming from overseas, with no warning.

In essence this allowed Outremer (as the Crusader States were often referred to by contemporaries, meaning literally 'beyond the sea') to punch above its weight. It was a small series of principalities facing a number of large, potentially hostile states. It should have been crushed in a few years, but this did not happen.

But there was a downside to this. The nobles who had travelled from Europe were there to gain glory against the infidel. They were bellicose and had no time to appreciate the finer things that were on offer. Some visitors looked down on the local Christian ruling elite as having 'gone native'. They were ready for action, so why not attack that Muslim stronghold just over there? The answer was quite often the rather surprising, 'They are our allies so no, please don't.'

This led to frictions, some of them quite intense, as we shall see later. However in the face of such an allegedly alien culture, the Christian lords very quickly fell into line with the realpolitik of the situation on the ground. But the nuances, the outside assistance, the papal decrees and also the increasingly powerful military orders led to dangerous bickering in front of powerful opponents. 'United we stand, divided we fall' was a lesson never learnt in the politics of Outremer.

Meanwhile, the Muslims were hardly more united. From their point of view, Al-Quds had fallen to barbarians and there was a novel new player at the table; but after the Christians' initial spectacular successes, the threat had been contained. Quite frankly, the Muslim princes were too distracted assessing each other's formidable potential to worry about the Franks scrabbling around on the edges of the Islamic world.

Again, this concept of a 'clash of civilisations' that has been used in the twenty-first century by extremist Muslim groups in the East and alarmist political parties in the West simply doesn't withstand close scrutiny. Nobody was trying to wipe out anyone – at least not yet. Battles were fought and betrayals occurred; but ultimately, this was a familiar scenario in the medieval world. If genuine crusaders were willing to negotiate with Muslim potentates and vice versa, than surely that's an applicable lesson for today.

There was one last political change in the region at this time, and that was the rise of the Hashashins, led by Hasan-i-Sabbah. The term *hashashin* is derogatory (meaning rabble, or, in today's parlance, yobs) and was never used by the sect. They called themselves the Nizari Ismaili; but the Arabic word *hashashin* has become the English word 'assassin'. They were despised partly because of their assassinations, but also because, as Ismailis, they were a separate sect of Islam, outside the Sunnis and Shi'as, so were often seen as the Islamic version of heretics. It is coincidence that the term sounds like the word 'hashish', and on that point the first job is to tackle a few myths about them.

Any secret religious society that goes around carrying out high-profile assassinations is likely to have some myths swirling around them. These stories were contemporary to the organisation and were created by both Muslims and Christians. Princes, warlords and generals of both cultures were targets for the Assassins, who often struck very publically, using knives coated in deadly poison. However, most of the sources were written by people outside of (and often targets of) the Nizari Ismaili.

My favourite myth (and one repeated by Marco Polo) is that to recruit new members, young initiates were taken to a castle where they were kept in the outer gatehouse and fed hash cakes. When sound asleep, the men were transferred into the main castle, where they awoke to find themselves surrounded by lush gardens, dancing girls and plentiful food and drink. After a few days of luxury and indulgence, they were again slipped some hash and, once in a stupor, returned to their starting point. When they awoke, they were informed by the Hashashins that they had experienced paradise and, in order to return, would have to follow orders and die martyrs to the cause.

It's an ingenious way of explaining the fanaticism and single-mindedness of these hitmen. It also explained their seemingly joyous response to being surrounded by the bodyguards of their high-profile victims and rapidly dispatched from this world. Of course, the modern reader will know it takes much less to brainwash young men into carrying out terrible acts of violence in the name of God.

This group embedded themselves in a string of castles in remote desert regions (mainly in modern-day Syria and western Iran). These were essentially impregnable as no army could realistically besiege a castle in such an arid region. This allowed the group to spread terror from safe bases. Hasan-i-Sabbah became known as 'the Old Man of the Mountains', and future rulers picked up the same title.

But they weren't the only ones in the assassination business in the Middle East. Both the crusaders and the

Muslim princes were responsible for their own fair share of murders, so the Hashashins' exact number of successful hits will probably never be known. In any case, because the sect was so secretive and because almost all our sources come from their enemies, it is hard to separate fact from fiction.

This aura of mystery and terror was exactly what they wanted; and while the Hashashins never deployed large armies or conquered vast territories, they were important players in the region for centuries. No person in power from Acre to Astrakhan was safe.

The County of Edessa, as mentioned above, was the first crusader state to be founded. As well as being one of the largest, it also stretched furthest east. Edessa was peppered with fortresses, so it was defensively sound and a formidable nut to crack, as Kerbogha had found.

The local population was largely composed of Orthodox Syrians and Armenians, and while they weren't the same as Catholic Christians they were at least more amenable to crusader rule than to Muslim overlords. Consequently, the Counts of Edessa could depend on popular support. However, by the 1130s there was a new generation on the scene, and the primary threat to Edessa was Imad ad-Din Zengi, known to all historians simply as Zengi. Through various power plays, Zengi was starting to unite and rule the disparate power bases in Syria. He became Atabeg (ruler) of Mosul in 1127. Then, just a year later, he was also ruling Aleppo; and while there was a Seljuk sultan on the scene, Zengi was in essence the ruler in the region. In 1130 he tried to intimidate the Governor of Damascus (partly through kidnapping his son). The ruse failed and resulted in the governor looking to the crusaders as an ally, employing the often-used logic that 'the enemy of my enemy is my friend'. Damascus became a buffer between Zengi and most of the Crusader States.

Meanwhile Zengi became somewhat fixated on the

Muslim city of Homs, besieging it on several occasions in the 1130s but always failing to capture it. The climax came in 1137 when the King of Jerusalem, Fulk, set out at the front of a crusader army to engage Zengi as he besieged the crusader castle of Baarin. Even though Zengi crushed this relief army and Fulk was forced to surrender and flee with the remnants of his force, Fulk had bought enough time for Damascus to muster its larger army. Zengi realised he couldn't afford to fight Damascus as well, so he made peace; and just in time, too, as Byzantium and another crusader army were heading towards him. This combined force laid siege to Zengi's fortress of Shaizar, where he had to rally his troops and break the siege, which he did successfully.

Zengi returned in 1138, having married a woman who conveniently came with the dowry of ... Homs, the city he'd been trying to take for nearly a decade. To add to his joyous wedding, he claimed that another part of the marriage deal was Damascus. Again, Damascus and the crusaders united to fend off the predatory Zengi. This Christian/Muslim alliance worked well and kept a friendly Muslim buffer state between the crusaders and Zengi. The exception was Edessa, which was easily the most exposed and potentially vulnerable of the Crusader States.

Since Zengi had already spent most of the 1130s in Syria and still failed to take Damascus, he began to look north for alternative conquests. All this was happening at a time when many disparate groups had shown unusual and effective cohesion (the Orthodox Byzantines, the Catholic crusaders and the Muslims of Damascus); but Joscelin II, Count of Edessa, knew nothing of this and had a massive falling out with the Count of Tripoli, the closest and most obvious Christian ally in the area around Edessa. As a result, when Zengi besieged the capital in 1144, nobody came to Joscelin's aid. The city fell, and effectively the entire county too. Edessa had been the very first Crusader State, and it was the first to fall to Muslim conquest.

The news spread back to Europe, and in December 1145 Pope Eugenius III issued the papal bull (decree) *Quantum Praedecessores*, which was a call for a second major crusade. The Pope used the greatest holy man of the time to help him spread the word of the crusade around France and Germany. Bernard of Clairvaux was a highly accomplished preacher and a man so otherworldly that nobody doubted him. Miracles seemed to follow him like his shadow, everywhere he went (he was made a saint after his death). Bernard's message of a second chance to take up arms and receive a full papal indulgence spread like wildfire. As before, there were massacres of Jewish communities in the Rhineland; but unlike last time, the crusading message spread to the highest in the land. This time the French king, Louis VII, and the German emperor, Conrad III, were to go with their own retinues. They were by no means the only countries represented, but the trip to the East was to be under French and German joint control.

This situation was hugely beneficial for almost everyone involved (except the Jews). Now Europe saw two of its most important monarchs taking on the spiritual commitment for God's battles against the infidel. It was also important for the Pope because throughout the Middle Ages (and later) the Pope was not just a spiritual leader, but also the ruler of a large area of central Italy. A number of popes in this era were more worried about temporal power than spiritual.

The situation was complicated by the issues around the Investiture Contest (for more on that, read my first book, *The Busy Person's Guide to British History*), which argued over whether it was the king or the Pope who ordained bishops. Suffice to say that throughout this period, the power of papal diplomatic pressure ebbed and flowed. However, having two of the most prestigious monarchs responding for the first time to a call for crusade boosted the Pope's standing enormously. It looked as if the Pope could order the German Emperor to do something, and he did it! It was, in the modern vernacular, a PR coup. Except that looks can be deceiving. The idea of a guaranteed eternity in heaven is not a hard sell. So on this occasion the Pope's interests and those of Louis and Conrad were the same. There were many times when that was not the case.

Most histories of the Second Crusade (1145–49) now go on to talk about the journey eastwards, but there were two important developments happening closer to home.

By the 1140s the concept of a target for the crusade was changing. While the southern Germans were happy to march east with Conrad, the northern German Christians asked Bernard of Clairvaux if they could instead fight the pagan Wends (Slavs) to the east. This request went all the way to Pope Eugenius, who issued a new papal bull, *Divina Dispensatione*, the first to offer the same absolution of sins that had been previously available only by going to Palestine. In this case, instead of fighting in the Holy Land, most of the action would take place in modern-day Poland.

This Northern Crusade consisted of Germanic princes as well as Scandinavian Christian rulers. They marched into enemy territory in 1147. Because of the vastly dissimilar terrain compared to that of Spain and the Middle East, this was a very different type of warfare. Instead of mountains and arid, sun-baked plains, there were dense, almost primeval forests. The settlements in this area were like islands in a sea of dark green. While the fighting was vicious, there were no grand pitched battles as in Dorylaeum or Ascalon. Instead it was a series of sieges in which civilian populations took the brunt of the violence. This Northern Crusade (it was never so called by contemporaries) ended in peace treaties, and the formal conversion of some Wends after one only campaigning season. In the short term the territorial gains of the Christians were limited, but the events of 1147 were significant for several reasons. Most importantly, they set a precedent; the fight against any unbelievers was now as sacred a cause as protecting the Holy Land. Secondly, and more practically, the looting, burning and pillaging across Pomerania (which was mainly pagan) led to significant depopulation, which was to weaken the pagans' resources in future conflicts.

This was the start of a long process of wars of conversion, because pretty much as soon as the crusaders left, most of the Wends returned to their pagan ways. As Bishop Albert of Pomerania summarised:

> If they had come to strengthen the Christian faith ... they should do so by preaching, not by arms.

A further important development was purely accidental. The English crusaders decided it would be much easier to get to the Holy Land by ship (an innovation in its own right). The expedition demonstrated the problem with this mode of transport and the mercurial nature of the sea. The ships were forced to land in Portugal, where King Alfonso requested the crusaders' help in besieging the mighty Moorish stronghold of Lisbon.

The crusaders agreed, and after a four-month siege, which largely involved encirclement and starving out the Muslim garrison, the Moors surrendered. This was another example of the expansionist Christian wars in Iberia becoming intertwined with the crusading movement. While Lisbon would eventually have fallen to the rising tide of Christian power at some point, its fall was accelerated by the Second Crusade. So the modern capital city of Portugal became Christian in 1147 and remains so to this day. Some of the English crusaders even stayed and settled in Lisbon, but many continued their journey.

So before the Second Crusade's main force had even entered the Middle East, it could already boast of two significant victories. This is important to remember when some historians point out an almost immediate diminishing of the returns on the investment in all subsequent crusades after the first one. With such a great start and both an emperor and a king leading armies east, surely the Second Crusade would have even greater success than the first.

Zengi, however, was not waiting for the crusaders when they arrived. In 1146 he was murdered by a Christian slave (not an assassin). His son Nur al-Din had to split Zengi's territory with his brother, but there was peace in the Syrian lands of the Muslims. This allowed Nur al-Din to pour all his time and effort into attacking crusader-held territory. Joscelin II had managed to scrape together an army to try and win back his county of Edessa, but he was not a great military leader and he lacked the resources to take on the Atabeg of Aleppo. Nur al-Din crushed him and Joscelin retreated in ignominy. Then the Muslim ruler cast his eye on the Principality of Antioch, which no longer had the shield of Edessa to protect it. When Nur al-Din captured a number of frontier castles, the Christian nobles were worried.

For the first time, a Muslim prince focused all his efforts on fighting the Christians. It's with Nur al-Din that we can first recognise that much-touted 'clash of civilisations'. He wanted to reconquer the lands the Christians had taken from the Muslims, and he carefully nurtured alliances with other Muslim warlords and princes to ensure that his efforts weren't sabotaged by an Islamic competitor.

The current governor of Damascus, Mu'in ad-Din Unur, had been a supporter of the crusader territories. He was one who enjoyed his autonomy and feared being absorbed by Nur al-Din's growing power. However, Nur al-Din was able to negotiate a treaty with Damascus, sealed when Nur al-Din married Mu'in ad-Din's daughter. While it did not make Mu'in ad-Din an active enemy of the Christians, it did at least weaken the links between Damascus and the Kingdom of Jerusalem. It does appear that Mu'in ad-Din remained suspicious of his new son-in-law.

Meanwhile, the French and Germans slowly made their way east. They marched through Byzantine lands and were meant to meet at Constantinople. When this didn't happen and the Germans arrived first, they were quickly moved on. From the point of view of the Byzantine emperors, the crusaders couldn't be trusted. Most armies at this time lived off the land, which meant that when large forces marched through agricultural areas they stripped them bare – sometimes paying for the food and animal fodder, but often not. The French dithered around Constantinople until the Byzantine Emperor at the time, Manuel I, lied to Louis that the Germans had secured a victory in Asia Minor, simply in order to get him to move off into Anatolia.

The Byzantines had stomached crusader armies the first time around, when they needed Western troops; however, the call for the Second Crusade had nothing to do with Byzantine wishes. They bitterly remembered that the First Crusade was meant to have returned Antioch to their control but that this hadn't happened. Ultimately, Louis and Conrad were treated as important but unwanted guests. Indeed, Manuel I was so suspicious of the approaching armies from the west that he even signed a truce with the Turkish sultanate of Rum in Anatolia. These two natural enemies effectively held their breath as the French and Germans were ushered out of Byzantine territory and into the realm of the Turks. Manuel I wanted all his troops near Constantinople in case the crusaders tried anything, a marked difference from the effective collaboration seen at the time of the First Crusade.

Conrad had badly misjudged his march through Anatolia. He had believed the hype around Manuel I and thought the

Byzantine Emperor had far more sway over the area than he really did. Conrad had also miscalculated distance, and so his army went through exactly the same traumas as the First Crusade. This time, however, the Turks were waiting for them. At the so-called Second Battle of Dorylaeum and another battle at Laodicea, Conrad's army suffered two humiliating defeats, and he was wounded into the bargain. All of this, plus the usual harsh central Anatolian terrain and climate, meant that by the time Conrad arrived in the Holy Land in 1148 most of his forces had deserted, been killed, or been captured and sold into slavery.

The French fared better. Although they suffered the same constant harassment from Turkish horse archers as they marched through Anatolia, there were only so many battles any force could fight in a campaigning season. The one-sided victories against the Germans meant the Turks were already bloated with booty, slaves and tales of martial prowess. Louis arrived in Outremer in better shape than Conrad, but the brutal trek from western Europe to the Holy Land seemed always to decimate the European armies.

Things actually got worse when Louis thought it was time to change tactics and decided to put his best men on ships to Antioch, sending the larger proportion of his troops on the comparatively short march from Adalia to Antioch. The plan completely backfired when the Turks attacked the sick and fatigued troops, so that on arrival at Antioch, Louis realised that he now had fewer than half the men he had set out with.

Most unusually, Louis travelled with his wife, Eleanor of Aquitaine (most crusaders, royal or otherwise, did not bring their spouses on such a dangerous and gruelling journey). It was in Antioch that Louis met Eleanor's uncle, Raymond of Poitiers. Raymond and Eleanor were delighted to see each other, in fact so delighted that it was rumoured that they had become a little too friendly and flaunted this in front of

Louis. This could be courtly gossip that has been preserved and passed down the centuries, but subsequent strains in the marriage do appear to start from this point. Curiously enough, it was Raymond who suggested that the crusade should attack Aleppo, a clever and intelligent strategy. This was Nur al-Din's stronghold and if they could capture that, the reconquest of Edessa, while not assured, would certainly be made much easier. Aleppo was a long way from friendly territory, but the concept was sound. Louis declined and quickly moved on from Antioch to Tripoli, and then to Jerusalem.

No self-respecting crusader is going to march from western Europe all the way to the Middle East and not go to Jerusalem. What's odd is that Eleanor seemed to take longer to get there than Louis and was accompanied, at least part of the way, by Uncle Raymond. To make matters worse for this travelling entourage of nobility, Alphonso, the Count of Toulouse, died on the way to Jerusalem. Raymond II, the Count of Tripoli, was accused of poisoning him (due to an old family feud); although nothing was ever proved conclusively, with no leader and a sudden feeling of being very unwelcome, Alphonso's much-needed troops boarded a fleet of ships and headed for home. These events show the genuine tensions and underlying divisions among the Christians.

It was with this kind of seething acrimony and animosity in the background that Conrad, Louis and Baldwin III, the King of Jerusalem, created the Council of Acre. In this coastal city the three monarchs, along with other key nobles and the Grand Masters of the Templars and Hospitallers, met to come up with a grand strategy for the crusading forces. It was a veritable who's who of the Christian aristocracy, half war council, half pageant. While on the surface everything looked fine and dandy, underneath was a disparate group, little concerned with looking at ways for Christianity to dominate Islamic states. They appeared simply to be trying to outdo one another in their petty interests. God's will seemed to be very low on the agenda.

A contemporary chronicler, William of Tyre, puts a better spin on things:

> They entered into a careful consideration as to what plan was the most expedient.

The target they came up with was Damascus, the same Damascus that had been an ally to the Christians. After what has already been written about the relationship between the crusaders and Damascus, this may sound surprising, and little wonder. While technically Mu'in ad-Din had become an ally of Nur al-Din, he was hardly an enthusiastic supporter. In the long term there could probably have been a diplomatic solution to the temporary changing of allegiances, particularly if the crusaders weakened Nur al-Din's power base.

But vanity had to have played its part. Conrad and Louis had travelled all this way and had risked so much to recapture Edessa. This plan was clearly not viable; and yet, while Aleppo would have been the sound strategic choice, how would that sound back home? Conrad, conqueror of a city you've never heard of ... that didn't seem to be worth all the effort. But Damascus – Damascus is in the Bible! St Paul was converted on the road to Damascus. This prize sounded much more suitable for a Christian military campaign.

It wasn't just the European kings who were keen on the idea. Baldwin III, still a teenager, was keen to escape from his domineering mother's shadow. He had been crowned in 1143, but his mother still acted as regent. However, if he was one of the monarchs to plant his flag on the towers of Damascus, his stock would rise substantially higher than his mother's. Consequently, a plan was hatched, a plan with the sole merit of massaging egos and one that made no strategic sense whatsoever. And so it was that the Second Crusade, which had been sent to bolster the defences of Christendom in the Holy Land, set out on a campaign that could only create more enemies and weaken the strategic viability of the Kingdom of Jerusalem. Not everyone was oblivious to this blunder, but everyone went along with it.

The Second Crusade set off towards Damascus in July, yet again during one of the hottest months of the year. Mu'in ad-Din had caught wind of this surprising development and did his best to make the journey to Damascus as uncomfortable as possible, taking away what food, shelter and water sources he could. He also took the opportunity to bolster the defences of the city and called on his son-in-law to come to his aid.

The crusade arrived on 24 July and promptly set up camp in the shady orchards on the edges of the city. These would at least be a comfortable base of operations. As in the siege of Antioch, the crusader army simply wasn't big enough to surround such a large city. Another war council assembled and, after further debate, the nobles of the Crusader States managed to convince Louis and Conrad that to move south-east of the city to a barren and scorched plain would be a tactically better option. It was a farcical suggestion; camping in a desert would never provide the supplies required for an army.

After four days of messing around on the outskirts of Damascus, having made no attempt to assault its walls, and with the news that Nur al-Din's relief army was closing in, the crusade raised the siege and headed back home. Folklore loves a brave defeat, and counterfactual history loves to look at 'what if?' – but there is nothing here apart from a terrible plan, executed in a lacklustre manner. While there were qualified successes that can be attributed to Pope

Eugenius's call for a crusade in Europe, the outcome for the principle forces in the Middle East was an unmitigated disaster.

Conrad raced back to Germany. Enough was enough. Louis spent more time in the Kingdom of Jerusalem, but he was gone by the summer of 1149. By 1154 Damascus had no option but to become a vassal state of Nur al-Din.

To quote William of Tyre again:

> From this time on the position of the Latins in the East deteriorated visibly.

With the buffer state of Damascus gone, the core coastal regions of the Crusader States were now up against a unified Islamic empire under Nur al-Din. And it wasn't just Damascus that was forced into his sphere of influence. In 1149 Mosul also came under his control. As Nur al-Din grew stronger and the Muslims of the Middle East became more unified, the exact opposite was happening in Outremer.

At first this didn't appear to be the case and it seemed William of Tyre was exaggerating, but only a little. Baldwin III grew into a brave leader, both feared and respected by Muslim and Christian princes alike.

Much of his reputation was sealed in the early 1150s. The problems arose from that other Islamic power base the Crusader States had to contend with: the Fatimid dynasty that ruled Egypt. Their main frontier base was Ascalon, which had been the site of the decisive Christian victory at the end of the First Crusade. Baldwin knew he couldn't take it in one go, so he rebuilt the town of Gaza and gave it to the Knights Templar to garrison. Now Baldwin had a secure base just ten miles from the key Fatimid fortress. His plans were put on hold when there was a brief civil war in the Crusader States as different interests vied for the throne of Jerusalem. I won't go into details because they are incredibly complex, but it's enough to say that there was constant jostling for any kind of advantage between the major factions in the Holy Land. This power struggle meant that the various groups sometimes deliberately did the wrong thing in terms of protecting Christian interests in the Middle East, in order to gain a short-term advantage over a rival. It's against such a backdrop that William of Tyre was writing, and you can see why he was so full of doom and gloom.

Baldwin won the brief war, showing he was a natural at both political and military manoeuvring; and in 1153, rallying every resource he could, he attacked Ascalon. This siege encompassed the great names of the Holy Land. It also showed what the Christians could do when unified. The Patriarch of Jerusalem brought the legendary fragment of the True Cross. The masters of the Templars and the Hospitallers were also there, as was the new Prince of Antioch, Raynald of Châtillon. Raynald had arrived in the Holy Land with Louis's forces during the Second Crusade. He came from minor nobility but married into the position of Prince of Antioch, something that many of the more established nobles (including Baldwin) did not support.

The siege lasted for five months. Unlike Damascus, it was vigorously executed. Coastal access was blocked by a crusader fleet, and siege towers were built to storm the walls. There were regular skirmishes and assaults. At one point, as one of the siege towers reached the walls, the defenders set it alight; but as the tower burned, it weakened the walls of Ascalon, causing a collapse.

An assault into the breach was beaten back after furious fighting, and in the ensuing melee the Grand Master of the Templars died. All looked lost, but three days later, the patriarch (with the omnipresent holy relic of the True Cross) told Baldwin to attempt a final assault; the Hospitallers agreed. This accord was enough to stop any wavering, and the final assault created another forced entrance into the fortress. This time the ferocity of the attackers took its toll on the exhausted defenders, and a permanent breach in the defences was made. The garrison formally surrendered and was allowed to leave for Egypt.

The siege of Ascalon was a major victory and ensured that an association between Nur al-Din and the Fatimids wouldn't happen anytime soon. Baldwin was quite rightly hailed as a hero, and the Christian states could breathe a little easier.

That is, until the following year when, as already mentioned, Nur al-Din captured Damascus. Over the next few decades the Fatimids had their own political upheavals, which bought the Christians some time. However, in 1156, Raynald of Châtillon claimed that the Emperor Manuel I had reneged on his promise to pay him a sum of money and vowed to attack Cyprus in retaliation. Unfortunately for him, the Latin Patriarch of Antioch refused to finance this expedition. Nobody believed Raynald, and by now he was getting a reputation for being a power-hungry opportunist with a sadistic streak. Nobody needed to make another enemy. An attack on Byzantine lands by the Prince of Antioch was about as good an idea as the Second Crusade besieging Damascus. However, Raynald lived up to his blossoming reputation and had the patriarch stripped naked, covered in honey and left in the sun on top of the citadel. He lay there on the hot, sun-baked roof with no water until he changed his mind. When the patriarch was released, he collapsed in exhaustion and agreed to finance Raynald's expedition. Raynald subsequently attacked Cyprus, ravaging the island and pillaging its inhabitants – and made another enemy in the process.

Raynald's luck ran out in 1160, while he was again plundering the Muslims and the Armenians. He was captured in a skirmish and sent to Aleppo, where he was held captive. As a result, one of Outremer's most volatile problems was put on hold for a while.

Meanwhile, Nur al-Din probed the Crusader States almost annually. Sometimes it was fortified towns; at other times his target was one of the many formidable castles of the military orders. Not every assault was victorious and not every exploratory attack was carried out with large forces, but while Nur al-Din could test the strength of his enemy, from the point of view of the Latin States, every time a Muslim army came into view it was potentially a moment of existential crisis.

Baldwin III died in 1163, and even Nur al-Din paused in memory of such a worthy foe; but hostilities soon began again, this time against the new leader, Amalric I. And so things ground on. However, Nur al-Din did not put all his efforts into attacking the crusaders; he expanded into the north and east against Muslim princes, too. There is a myth about most of the Muslim opponents of the crusaders in the Middle East which says that they only engaged in Muslim versus Christian battles. In the later case of Saladin, he undoubtedly spent more time in the saddle fighting Muslim foes than Christian ones.

Examples of this can also been seen in the far west. By this period, just over half of the Iberian Peninsula was Christian; however, the Muslim princes faced a dangerous new enemy, not from the various Christian principalities in the north, but from the south and a group of Berber Muslims known as the Almohads. By the time Nur al-Din died in the East, the Christians faced a more formidable and unified foe in the West. The Almohads ruled much of north-western Africa (north of the Sahara) and absorbed the Muslim principalities of Spain into that sphere of influence. None of the Spanish and Portuguese princes had anything like the resources that the Almohad Caliphate could muster.

Despite the fact that the Christians were fighting on,

Islam was in the ascendancy on all the fronts. Nur al-Din died of a fever in Damascus in 1174, just as he was on the cusp of assaulting and potentially absorbing the Fatimids into his empire. Nur al-Din's family would have continued the struggle, but a peaceful coup was carried out by Salah al-Din Yusuf ibn Ayyub, the son of one of Nur al-Din's generals and a man forever remembered as Saladin. Saladin was a Sunni Kurd who was sent to work with the Shi'a Fatimids. He was highly regarded in this alien court and eventually became vizier. In 1178, with the death of the caliph, he effectively took over Egypt and allied it to the Abbasid Caliphate of modern-day Iraq. When Nur al-Din died, it was from this power base that Saladin headed north into Syria and quickly took the core of his empire.

There was more to be done, and he went to war with the governors of Aleppo and Mosul. After victory there, he was proclaimed Sultan of Egypt and Syria, a position of power unheard of since the very first Islamic caliphate, 500 years earlier. This concentration of power made everyone on the edges of it nervous. The Crusader States looked on in horror and the Assassins, realising that they were now minnows living next to a very hungry shark, tried to assassinate him twice, failing on both occasions.

It is at this point that Raynald of Châtillon returns to the story. He had languished in prison for over sixteen years until he was ransomed for 120,000 gold dinars in 1176. Raynald may have been merciless, but sometimes that's just what is required when facing a dangerous enemy. One of Saladin's first attacks on Outremer led to the epic Battle of Montgisard. Saladin had a massive army of about 26,000, while the Christians managed to muster an army of a few thousand, supported by 500 Knights Templar. The leader was the sixteen-year-old Baldwin IV. Having a boy as a king at a time of crisis is never a good thing. What was worse was that Baldwin IV was a leper, so he stood no chance of having children; he was slowly becoming less mobile as his enemy grew ever stronger. So it was up to Reynald's sheer bloody-mindedness, backed by the elite Templars, to save the day.

Saladin knew the forces Baldwin could field were tiny compared to those he had carefully organised. Saladin was hoping for a surgical strike, cutting through Christian-held lands and heading straight for Jerusalem. Tired of being seen as a usurping Kurd, he believed this prize would validate him as a 'ghazi', a holy warrior. He sent just a detachment of his troops to convince Baldwin that the rest of his army faced no real threat.

As the march continued, Saladin's army spread out to forage for food and got distracted by the odd village here and there. Meanwhile, in an unbelievable display of single-mindedness, Raynald arrived on the scene, apparently from out of nowhere, prepared to attack. The Christians were outnumbered ten to one, but they were in battle-ready formation and had the element of surprise. Saladin's army was spread out over miles, tired from the forced march.

Baldwin ordered the holy relic of the True Cross to be raised, after which he was helped down from his horse to pray. The imagery of a boy king, ravaged by disease and showing such piety, must have been inspiring. Following brief prayers, the knights remounted and charged across the sand at the utterly chaotic Muslim lines.

The battle was over before it had begun. The crusader force smashed into the ranks of Saladin's men. Baldwin was seen in the thick of the fight, arms bandaged, determined to swing a sword and defend his kingdom. Saladin's force dissolved and disappeared; he had miscalculated utterly, and instead of marching a victorious army all the way to Jerusalem, he was now forced to flee for his life. After suffering ten days of heavy rain (a very rare event in Palestine), Saladin made his way back to Egypt. The whole sequence of events had a kind of surreal quality. It is thought that Saladin lost 90 per cent of his men in battle, in the rainstorm or during subsequent Bedouin attacks on his fleeing forces. There was personal loss, too, as his own nephew died in the battle.

By contrast, Baldwin, Raynald and the Templars returned as heroes. It was one of the most monumental victories in history, and yet the battle itself has been largely forgotten. This is mainly because the ridiculous mismatch in army size tells the real story. Be it divine intervention or luck, the Christians were now facing a monster and had no real defences against it. If the Battle of Montgisard was a miracle, they would need a regular supply of them to have any chance of survival against Saladin.

The battle did buy the Christians time though. Saladin was normally quite a shrewd and careful commander, so to have had one of his bolder moves end in such humiliating catastrophe brought about a more cautious approach and, eventually, a temporary truce with the Kingdom of Jerusalem. That four-year cessation of hostilities also allowed him to mop up the few remaining independent Muslim princes in Syria, although he never succeeded in capturing Mosul.

While Saladin was concentrating on absorbing the remaining Islamic principalities around Syria, things were relatively quiet on the Muslim and Christian borders. There was one exception: Raynald had now carved out a territory for himself on the hinterland between the Kingdom of Jerusalem and Saladin's lands. His key position of power was Crac des Chevaliers, a very safe base of operations for him. Raynald had a habit of attacking civilian caravans and even pilgrims on the way to Mecca, an act that disgusted all Muslims. Baldwin sent a message to Saladin that these actions were not sanctioned by him, that Raynald was an unruly subject acting on his own. Saladin tried attacking Crac, but when the fortress proved too strong, he went on to more pressing matters. It was enough for Saladin for the time being.

In 1182, not content with attacking Muslim pilgrims journeying to Mecca, Raynald launched ships into the Red Sea and carried out raids near the holy city itself. It could be argued either that he was taking the fight to the enemy, or that he was a violent warmonger whose bloodlust could never be sated. Either way, in late 1186, he attacked another large pilgrim caravan, which broke the explicit terms of the current truce. This was the final straw for Saladin. Raynald's attacks amounted to little more than mosquito bites, but a mosquito can become annoying. Saladin declared that the truce was over and went to war against all of the Crusader States, vowing that if he captured Raynald he would personally behead him.

For the Kingdom of Jerusalem the war couldn't have come at a worse time. Baldwin IV had died two years earlier and was succeeded by another boy king, Baldwin V; but by 1187 he was dead, too. Baldwin V's regent, Guy de Lusignan, now tried to claim the throne, but he was not alone. Just as Saladin was bearing down with an army of 30,000, the Crusader States were once again bickering among themselves with factions vying for power. Personal gain overrode any kind of Christian unity, and yet the only way to survive this onslaught was solidarity.

Guy's chief problems were that he claimed the throne only through his wife Sibylla's line and that he was a relative newcomer to the realm. While he had the best claim (even if it was fairly tenuous), he had no real power base. The main rival faction belonged to Raymond of Tripoli, who represented the established nobility of Outremer. These factions were close to open war as Saladin arrived with his army on the borders of the Crusader States. This time Saladin was well prepared and had a plan.

Saladin looked to split his enemy and brokered a deal

with Raymond. Just as Saladin entered Galilee, Bailian of Ibelin, a respected Christian noble working on behalf of Guy de Luisignan, was warned by Raymond to stay away from the area. Bailian ignored the warning, and he and his entourage were captured by Saladin. This setback provided the impetus which forced Guy and Raymond to reconcile. Did they still have the time for another miracle?

The perennial problem the kings of Jerusalem faced was a lack of manpower. There were enough men to defend and protect the walled cities and fortresses of the Holy Land, or there were enough men to muster a formidable and well-armed army. But there were not enough men to do both. The Christians were always one major defeat away from disaster. Fortunately, any defeats they had suffered over the recent decades had been skirmishes in which not enough men were lost to cause serious harm. But in an attempt to match Saladin's numbers, Guy and Raymond mustered all the available manpower, bolstering their regular forces with the elite heavy cavalries of the Templars and the Hospitallers. In total, they had a force of around 20,000.

Saladin understood the crusaders' dilemma, and he knew he had to compel them to fight before they could retreat behind the thick walls of their many citadels, after which it would take decades to defeat them. But if he could lure them into a decisive battle, then he would become the conqueror of the Holy Land. The crusader army waited in the safety and shade of the springs of Suffuriya while assessing Saladin's movements. When Saladin besieged the fortress of Tiberias, he was not after Tiberias itself, but what was in it. Her name was Eschiva, and she was Raymond of Tripoli's wife.

The crusaders met in a war council. Saladin was close, but his army had been broken in two: the force besieging Tiberias and the rest as a standing army. Was this the time to attack? Raymond heard news of a breach in the walls of Tiberias in which some of the garrison had been killed and others taken prisoner. How long could his wife and her guards hold out? Everyone knew that if they got this wrong, it could mean the end of the Crusader States. Raynald was present at the council, and as usual he called for action and battle.

It is unclear what exactly swayed the council, but it took the bait and headed off to battle. Saladin had learned a lot in the eleven years since the Battle of Montgisard. In that situation he had underestimated his opposition, had been surprised by them and fought in an area not of his choosing. He made none of those mistakes on this occasion. This time Saladin made sure that all the wells had been poisoned and that his men had set fire to the shrubs and vegetation in the area. The crusaders, marching in their heavy mail armour and steel helmets, must have been gasping for water. The July furnace of Palestine was intensified now by choking smoke and wild bush fires. The heat must have been unbearable.

On 4 July the armies finally met on the slopes of the Hattin. The mountain of Hattin has two peaks which look like devil horns; under them, Saladin and his army were waiting for the parched and tired crusaders. As they had done at Mongisard, the Christians carried before them the relic of the True Cross, and they had mustered the greatest crusader army anyone had seen in a generation in the Holy Land. They also knew that an effective charge from the heavy cavalry could shatter the lightly armoured Muslims.

This was the moment of truth. The Hospitallers, Templars and nobles of the land charged forwards, a wall of steel. With the heat of high summer and a lack of water, the heavy cavalry had a chance for one great charge to shatter the Muslims, or perish themselves. As the cavalry galloped towards the Muslim light cavalry, the sun glinting off their helmets, their banners snapping smartly in the wind, it looked as though Saladin might have, once again, made a terrible mistake. Could his forces withstand such a hammer blow?

But light cavalry are easily manoeuvred, and the plain around the mountain gave plenty of scope for movement. As the Christian knights charged up the slopes of Hattin, exhausting themselves in the process, the Muslims merely parted their cavalry, opening like a giant set of sliding doors. The crusaders were unable to change course and charged straight into the gap.

Once past the main body of light cavalry, Saladin closed the gates and reformed his army. Now the spent crusader cavalry was cut off from the rest of their forces. Their gamble had not paid off; they were looking at total destruction.

The Muslim horse archers did what they did best: circling the crusader cavalry and infantry, they loosed volley after volley of arrows. A hailstorm of steel descended on the exhausted and thirsty Christian soldiers. Of the 20,000 or so in the Christian army, only about 3,000 escaped death or imprisonment. It was a tactical and strategic killer blow for Outremer, which now faced annihilation. More than just men were lost at Hattin: their king was captured, the Bishop of Acre died in the battle and the True Cross was now in enemy hands.

After the slaughter, Saladin had some of the most important prisoners brought to his tent. He handed Guy a refreshing drink. Giving a captive food at this time signified that he would be taken care of and would not face execution. Guy passed the cup to Raynald, who was kneeling next to him. Enraged by this, Saladin knocked the cup out of Raynald's hands, saying he was an oath breaker. Raynauld replied nonchalantly, 'Kings have always acted thus, I did no more.'

With that, Saladin grabbed Raynald and beheaded him just outside the tent, so ending one of the bloodiest careers in crusader history (and that is saying something). Guy was terrified that he was next, but Saladin calmed him. While most of the prisoners were sold into slavery, Saladin made sure anyone wearing the symbols of the military orders was executed. He didn't need any of those fanatics coming back to fight another day.

Because Guy had gambled everything, the Battle of Hattin was one of the most pivotal in medieval history. The Christians now had almost no men to hold any of their strongholds. Rarely does one battle unlock an entire kingdom, but that's what Hattin did for Saladin.

It was also important because it shows something about the personality of Saladin. He was a warrior and did not shy away from shedding blood, but he was also smart and had a sense of chivalry, traits which were to help him in the coming months. In fact, the very next day he rode to Tiberias, where the countess surrendered immediately, knowing that there was no point in resisting any further and that when Saladin guaranteed safe passage, he meant it. This pattern would be repeated again and again; he would offer terms, the city or castle would open its doors and the Christians would leave, all with minimal or no bloodshed.

It was late September when Saladin arrived at Jerusalem, defended then by the queen and Bailian of Ibelin, with just a few thousand soldiers to face an army of 20,000. While the city had no chance of relief, Saladin could always get more men. The siege of Jerusalem in 1187 was unlike the one in 1099; there were bloody assaults, but time was on the besiegers' side.

Saladin had come prepared. The Muslims had learned from the Christians; Saladin used the European invention of the siege tower (a massive timber structure that was rolled against the walls of a castle or city), along with catapults that pounded the walls, and Greek fire (a mysterious compound, a kind of medieval napalm) to burn down defensive positions. Just over a week into the siege, Saladin had shown a knack for another form of offensive siege warfare – tunnelling. On 28 September part of the city wall was undermined and collapsed. While the Christians fought bravely, discussions for the peaceful surrender of the city continued. Saladin was demonstrating a classic example of the carrot and the stick. The longer the crusaders held out, the more miserable things would become and the smaller their chances were of leaving with their lives.

While thousands died and Saladin displayed an almost textbook knowledge of siege assault, it's telling that a deal was struck by 2 October, less than two weeks after his arrival. There is documentation showing that Saladin toyed with the idea of massacring the Christian population. This tarnishes his almost whiter-than-white image in the popular imagination, but he had already demonstrated a ruthless streak when it mattered. What's important is that, no matter what he was thinking, it was his actions that counted and the population remained unmolested. When he discovered that many poor Christians could not meet his tax demand to keep them from slavery, he let them go.

It's worth comparing the Muslim conquest of 1187 with the Christian one of 1099. The earlier of these was almost within living memory of the latter, and yet the two events couldn't have been more different. When the Christians entered their most holy city, they descended into an orgy of bloodletting. Carcases were piled high and the city depopulated; the resulting charnel house reeked of the stench of death for months. But after this brief siege, Saladin placed his banner on the city walls and it was largely business as usual. In Jerusalem's long history, this was one of the most peaceful outcomes of a siege.

And so Saladin's march westward continued. In a now familiar pattern, he would ride up to the next Christian stronghold, and after a negotiation he would gain entrance.

When he came to the mighty city of Acre, the same thing happened. Saladin appeared unstoppable ... except there was a flaw in his strategy: the Christians had to go somewhere. Maybe he assumed they would head back to Europe, in which case he was very much mistaken. The coastal city of Tyre became the destination for Christian men, women and children. Tyre didn't have much of an army, but it had more than enough motivated and well-armed men to defend it. Saladin had inadvertently created an impregnable crusader citadel.

He tried attacking it, but failed. Tyre was too well defended, and Saladin's troops were exhausted from the speed of his campaigning. The balance of power couldn't remain like this indefinitely, but for the moment the Christians and Muslims existed in an uneasy stalemate. In the meantime, the loss of Jerusalem reverberated around Europe, along with increasingly desperate reports of Saladin's never-ending gains in the Holy Land. When the news reached the Pope and the nobility of Europe, there could only be one possible response: the Third Crusade was born.

Eleanor of Aquitaine was the only queen to go on crusade when she had followed her husband, King Louis VII of France, on the Second Crusade. However, as already discussed, their marriage was an unhappy one. After Louis returned to France, he managed to further alienate most of his subjects, as well as the Pope. Shaving off his beard was the last straw for Eleanor, who now found him unbearably ugly as well as overly pious (she once said she had hoped to marry a king, but instead had married a monk). She got a divorce (in the medieval era, for a woman to get a divorce – and from a king, no less – was almost unheard of) and left Louis, taking her dowry of the Duchy of Aquitaine, a massive slice of western France, nearly a fifth of the modern country. Whom was she to marry next? The answer is the English king, Henry II.

Henry and Eleanor had many children, including a son called Richard. This vibrant and bellicose young man was to inherit more than just Eleanor's lands; he, like her (and Henry II), had a forceful personality. He was not afraid of a fight; some would say that he was foolishly brave, but by the age of sixteen he had already earned a reputation as a fierce warrior.

4

Legends Are Born: The Third Crusade

It was Pope Gregory VIII who formally declared the Third Crusade (1189–92); in a masterstroke he informed Europe that Jerusalem had been lost as God's punishment for all the sinful things Christian Europe had been doing. By now the routine of rallying a crusade fitted a standard pattern, and impassioned messages echoed from the pulpits of Europe. Gregory further declared a 'Saladin Tithe', a special tax on both laymen and clergy to pay for this monumental undertaking.

The news of Jerusalem's fall had so shocked the current French king, Philip Augustus, and the English king, Henry II, that they stopped their war with each other and swore to go on crusade. This was music to Gregory's ears; war in France would prevent some of the potential key players from joining the crusade. Besides, shouldn't Christians be fighting the infidel rather than each other? But Henry died in 1189, leaving his son Richard to take the cross and become a crusader. This was a young warrior who, because of his military leadership and prowess, had already won the title of Richard the Lionheart (Richard Coeur de Lion).

While Richard and Philip were to take armies to the Holy Land, these were to be dwarfed by the endeavours of the German Emperor, Frederick Barbarossa (Red Beard). Frederick had been a young man in the retinue of Conrad on the Second Crusade. Now, as an old and all-powerful emperor, he was determined to get things right on this second attempt. The French and English mustered 8,000–10,000 men each, whereas Frederick gathered a colossal army of about 100,000. This was probably the largest army Europe had seen since the Roman era, possibly the largest ever. France and England were going to have to play second fiddle to Barbarossa.

What Richard lacked in sheer manpower, he made up for in military thinking. Richard had drawn the conclusion that marching armies from Europe to the Middle East was a slow and dangerous strategy. Better to sail there. True, the sea had its own dangers, but they were hardly greater than constant harassment through enemy territory, hoping that with a little bit of luck, or God's blessing, you could arrive in the Holy Land with your forces more or less intact. It's worth noting that Richard went to all the trouble of planning and spending vast fortunes, knowing that he would be lucky to gain any glory under the shadow of Barbarossa.

Richard took his fleet via Sicily where, as a result of dynastic feuding, his sister had been imprisoned. Richard was determined to rectify this state of affairs, so when he arrived with his crusader army, they besieged Messina. The situation was rapidly resolved and his sister was freed. This wasn't a major conflict between a Christian territory and crusaders, but Richard was misusing his crusaders (who had been paid for largely by the Church) to fight Christians rather than Muslims, which was the wrong way round.

It was also here that Richard fell out with Philip Augustus when, instead of marrying Philip's half-sister, he married Berengaria of Navarre (an English queen you've never heard of). After this detour, Richard's fleet continued eastwards. It was near Cyprus that what he had dreaded happened: his fleet was battered by a storm. Only a few ships ran aground; however, they were key vessels carrying his sister, his wife and most of his treasury. Later, when the wrecks were inspected, all the bodies of the crew were found, but the women and gold were missing. It didn't take long to discover that the culprit was Isaac Komnenos, the ruler of Cyprus and technically a vassal of the Byzantine Emperor. Richard made straight for Limassol, where he confronted Isaac.

Isaac wanted to get Richard out of his home city, so he returned the women and the gold and even promised troops for the crusade. However, as soon as Richard left, Isaac went back on nearly everything he had said, at which point the laws of nature took over. When a sheep antagonises a wolf, there's no contest. Richard seized Cyprus within days, and Isaac was taken prisoner. Richard had not planned a Christian conquest of Cyprus; it was already Christian land under the authority of Byzantium. But it was now a crusader territory under the authority of the Western Church, and not the emperor in Constantinople. As a result of Richard's legacy, Cyprus was to become one the biggest thorns in the side for all Muslim leaders for many centuries to come. Even as the mainland was lost forever to the Christians, Cyprus would remain a Christian stronghold up until the era of the Ottomans.

Meanwhile, Frederick had been slogging across Europe, doing things the old-fashioned way. The First Crusade's genesis had been in part created by the Byzantine Empire, and until Antioch, for large periods of that campaign East and West had worked relatively well together. It is therefore interesting to note that by the Third Crusade, the Byzantine Emperor, Isaac II Angelos, instead of supporting Frederick's progress through Anatolia, made a secret alliance with Saladin to impede Frederick's progress.

However, in the hinterland between Isaac's lands and Saladin's realm, the Turkish sultanate of Rum reached out to the German crusading army and promised Frederick safe passage through Anatolia. But the Turks just couldn't help themselves, and the classic pattern of horse archer ambushes/skirmishes happened again and again. Unsurprisingly, Frederick lost patience and the German army sacked Iconium, the capital city of the Sultanate. This bought him some peace and also demonstrated how efficient his massive army could be. It would have been a huge asset to the Christians hanging on in Tyre.

Unfortunately, in June 1190, while crossing a river in eastern Anatolia, Frederick's horse lost its footing, slipped, and both rider and horse fell into the water. The shock of the accident was fatal to the sixty-eight-year-old Frederick. The leader of the largest-ever crusading army lay dead by the side of an innocuous river hundreds of miles away from the Holy Land and 1,000 miles away from home. His nobles attempted to pickle him, to preserve him for the journey home, but the process was flawed and his remains reeked. He was buried in Antioch.

To say this was a disaster for the Third Crusade is an understatement. Its leader was dead and his carefully prepared and massive army quickly dissolved, the vast majority of men heading home while mourning the loss of one of the greatest Holy Roman Emperors. Now all hopes rested on those bitter rivals: the King of France and the (still largely untested) King of England, each with tiny armies compared to Frederick's monstrous force.

However, there was a tiny glimmer of hope in these tangled circumstances. The local Christians had been keeping themselves busy with a siege of Acre. This meant that the first goal of the crusade was defined and already prepared. Perhaps the added forces of Philip and Richard could tip the balance in the Christians' favour?

The siege of Acre is one of those epic ones that occasionally come up in history. Acre was always a tough nut to crack.

Sitting as it did on a peninsula, it could be resupplied by sea and had formidable defences facing the land. The siege had already been dragging on for two years by the time the French and English kings arrived. There had been pitched battles and, even more unusually, Saladin had managed to surround the Christian besiegers, so they themselves were now under siege. Resistance from all sides was ferocious, and no matter how many men Saladin had thrown at the crusaders in attempt to relieve the city, he had failed to do so. He had missed his opportunity, and two fresh armies were now on the scene.

Disease is always a danger during a siege, and in this case malaria and malnourishment were two major causes of death. As usual, the Christian leadership had been split into various feuding factions, slowing any cohesive strategy against Acre and Saladin. This changed with the arrival of the European monarchs. Philip arrived first and built trebuchets (an improvement over the catapult and the most powerful pre-gunpowder artillery in history). These massive machines of war began to tear holes in the substantial walls of Acre. Soon afterwards, with the arrival of King Richard, there was an attempt to meet with Saladin, during which a three-day truce was to be agreed. Unfortunately, both Richard and Philip fell ill, and the meeting did not take place.

So the trebuchets continued their work, and a deadly game of cat and mouse developed. When a breach in the walls was large enough for a crusader assault, Saladin countered with an attack on the Christians, giving the besieged garrison just enough time to repair the breach. But this couldn't go on forever, and after a major assault carried out by the Christians was repelled in a bloody fight at the walls of the city on 3 July, the city offered its formal surrender on the 4th. Surprisingly, Richard declined the surrender, demanding better terms for the crusaders. On

11 July there was one final battle, and while the Christians were still unable to dislodge Saladin, the city surrendered a second time on the 12th. Conrad of Montferrat was given the honour of raising the banners on the city wall. He chose to raise the flags of the kingdoms of Jerusalem, France, England and the Duchy of Austria.

The last banner mentioned was contentious, to say the least. Leopold V of Austria had demanded the same honours as the three kingdoms on the grounds that he represented the remaining German contingent; and while only a count, he had (in theory) imperial status as a representative of the late Frederick. Richard fundamentally disagreed with this and had Leopold's banner torn down, a humiliation that neither Leopold nor Conrad would ever forget.

Because of this slight, Leopold (and his contingent) left in a huff immediately after the siege had finished. Philip Augustus was not far behind. He had probably wanted to stay, but succession disputes in France threatened his authority, and as a young king he wanted to have an actual kingdom to go home to. So Philip left, although a significant number of his troops remained in the Holy Land. As the other leaders ebbed away, Richard found himself in sole charge of the Christian expeditionary forces, but with the departure of his main rival the clock was now ticking on his own time in Outremer.

Saladin was all too aware of this and, after such a major defeat at Acre, became the master of delaying tactics over the fate of the garrison. The negotiations for their release dragged on for over a month. When Richard finally lost his patience, he marched all 2,700 of the Muslim prisoners out into the hinterland between the city and Saladin's army. Here, in full view of Saladin and his forces, Richard ordered the decapitation of each and every one of them. Saladin couldn't save them and responded by killing all of the Christian prisoners he had.

Richard's cold-blooded performance showed Saladin that cheap tricks weren't going to work. This was not a frenzied massacre in the style of the First Crusade's sacking of Jerusalem, but a calculated act. Had Saladin really wanted the safety of the garrison, he'd had ample time to ensure it. Had Richard wanted only to eradicate the garrison, why wait a month? The massacre of these 2,700 unarmed prisoners was a declaration of intent. Richard was nobody's fool, and he would not work to anyone's schedule but his own.

But time was pressing on Richard as he led his army south along the coast towards another important port at Jaffa. Saladin's light cavalry harassed them all along the route. He needed to break the formations of the Christians because their heavy armour and large shields meant that, as units, they were largely impregnable to Turkish bows. Richard knew this and was determined to march in strict battle order as the end of the journey would invariably lead to another siege. By marching along the coast, he could be resupplied by sea and also ensure that Saladin could not surround him. It was another example of Richard's iron will made manifest.

Eventually, the attacks took their toll. On 7 September, as the army moved through a wooded area near Arsuf, the Hospitaller heavy cavalry could take no more, broke from the rest of the army and charged the Muslims. This left Richard in a dilemma. He could sacrifice this elite heavy cavalry and keep the cohesion of his force, or he could start a full scale battle at a place not of his choosing. He picked the latter and quickly supported the Hospitallers with everything he had.

Saladin knew that the temporarily separated Hospitallers were vulnerable, and he himself joined the battle to encourage their destruction. But the rapid response by the European heavy cavalry meant the Muslims had strayed too close and were too tightly packed. The result was like a sledgehammer hitting a watermelon. Saladin's forces were thrown into disarray as the Muslims were outclassed in close-quarter combat with the Christian knights. The light cavalry was now an easier target and the European crossbow, while tortuously slow to reload, could effortlessly pierce the light Muslim armour. Horses and riders were felled with volley after volley of accurate fire.

As Saladin's forces began to flee the battlefield, Richard showed his tactical worth in the last acts of this battle. He knew the Muslims sometimes feigned retreat, only to return stronger; he also knew that as his army chased down Saladin's men they would lose their all-important cohesion. In short, if he wasn't careful, victory could be turned into a last-minute defeat. He stopped the pursuit and had the crusaders regroup and move on. The crusade had lost less than 1,000 men, whereas Saladin probably lost about a third of his force.

The Battle of Arsuf was another key victory for the Third Crusade. Had Saladin won, that would have been the end of the expedition. It was as simple as that. Saladin had suffered a humiliating defeat and there was no way he was going to risk another battle, at least not until Richard reached Jaffa. The port had heard about the fall of Acre and the battle at Arsuf and capitulated almost immediately when the crusade arrived. Now Richard looked towards the ultimate goal of all these exertions: Jerusalem.

Saladin had tried defeating Richard in a siege and failed. He had tried outmanoeuvring him with the judicious use of prolonged negotiations and failed. He had tried to ambush him in the traditional way and failed. Finally, he had tried the risky strategy of a pitched battle and failed. Could nothing stop this young warrior king?

Richard turned his army away from the coast and headed inland towards Jerusalem. The army marched to Beit Nuba, a small town only a dozen miles from the holy city. As the Christians got ever closer to their prize, Saladin's situation was becoming worse. The feudal duties of some of his army had been fulfilled, so chunks of it were peeling off and heading home. Morale in Saladin's army and in Muslim Jerusalem was leaking away.

At what seemed to be his bleakest moment, Saladin could not foresee the two things that would halt the crusader juggernaut. Firstly, the weather was unseasonably cold and wet; it was not good marching weather. Secondly, Richard was not just a fearless leader but a smart tactician, too. The unthinkable was being discussed in the crusader camp: should an assault even be attempted? The crusader leaders knew that Saladin was on the back foot and that now was the time to strike. There would be no better opportunity. However, to Richard's credit, he also realised that while capturing Jerusalem was easy, holding it would be a much harder proposition. Was it worth spilling blood, only for Jerusalem to be recaptured as soon as Richard set off for home? Once again, we see a situation where these supposedly zealous crusaders showed a surprising level of pragmatism; and once again, we witness supposedly intractable enemies engaging in diplomacy rather than war. It's also interesting to note that further scheming in the crusader camp showed a distinct lack of Christian brotherhood during a time of holy war. Richard backed Guy to be king, while nearly everyone else wanted Conrad. When it was put to a vote, Conrad, unsurprisingly, won (Guy was given Cyprus in compensation); however, before Conrad had time to even sit on the throne, he was murdered by two Assassins. While this was technically a Muslim-on-Christian murder, the target was so partisan that it was widely accepted that Richard was the one who had hired the Assassins – a Christian king at the head of a crusade paying Muslim hitmen to take out an elected Christian king. *Deus Vult*?

The negotiations between Richard and Saladin (who never actually met) dragged on, but one of Saladin's concessions was to allow any of the crusaders who wanted to do so to go on pilgrimage to Jerusalem. Richard refused, saying he could never look at the city he couldn't capture. The situation was drifting until, in July 1192, Saladin tried one last roll of the dice against the Lionheart. He gathered a small army and assaulted Jaffa, quickly regaining that key city. Richard had been outmanoeuvred.

In typical Lionheart style, rather than slowly raising his whole army to action, Richard picked the cream of his soldiers, the elite, and with these 2,000 men raced down the coast in ships and assaulted the numerically superior forces in the walled city of Jaffa. There is a description of Richard leaping down into the surf, clad in mail armour, a sword in one hand and a crossbow in the other. The speed and ferocity of the attack took the Muslims completely by surprise. They panicked and fled. In one campaign Richard had shown an ability to coordinate a siege, a full-scale battle and a skirmish. On the other hand, Saladin, that usually highly efficient military commander, was made to look weak.

This was the last major engagement of the Third Crusade. As he headed home, Richard ran into Leopold, the Austrian count he had insulted by taking down his banner at the siege of Acre. Leopold captured Richard and subsequently ignored a papal warning to release him, while at the same time accepting payments from both Prince John and Philip Augustus (who outbid Eleanor of Aquitaine) to keep him incarcerated for years. A caged lion seemed safer to many. After finally being released, Richard was in the process of crushing Philip's power in France when a million-to-one shot by a boy from a minor castle at a tiny siege killed one of the great legends of the crusading movement.

The First Crusade is seen as a clear win for the Christians, and it was. The Second Crusade was a clear loss for them (in the East undoubtedly; in the West, it did achieve a lasting legacy). The Third Crusade is often referred to as a 'draw'. It's not just crass to equate sporting analogies to holy war, it's also wrong. Had the Third Crusade failed in the Holy Land as spectacularly as the Second Crusade, Saladin would have wiped any Christian influence in the Middle East from the face of the earth forever. The Crusades would never have become ingrained in Western culture as these heroic endeavours; instead, they would have been one of the more obscure points of medieval history.

With a small amount of help from Frederick and Philip, Richard the Lionheart built on already firm foundations. From the brink of defeat, Outremer, while diminished in size, was a going concern once again. Jerusalem was lost, but Acre, Jaffa and Ascalon had all been recaptured and refortified. And it's important to remember that Cyprus, so often overlooked, was captured by the Third Crusade (albeit from Byzantium, rather than a Muslim foe) and was to remain a Western Christian outpost into the Renaissance. The Third Crusade was no draw, but a major success for the crusading movement.

Up until this point in the story of the Crusades, the major crusades had each been separated by a generation. Several decades would pass before a new crusade was preached. However, after the Third Crusade, crusading itself became something of an industry, with shorter gaps between them, and in some cases with crusades overlapping. While there had been regular crusading activity for over a century on all three fronts – the Middle East, Spain and northern Europe – it was only now that numbered crusades were going to be called for, again and again.

5

War Crimes: The Fourth Crusade

The Crusader States in the Middle East had always had a symbiotic relationship with trade. Spices and exotic fruits such as dates and figs, along with silks and other luxuries, could fetch high prices in the West, while European staples found ready markets in the East. The principle traders were the two great rival powers of Genoa and Venice, and it was their interests (though mainly Venice's) in the East that would cause all sorts of problems for the Fourth Crusade.

The Fourth Crusade (1202–1204) was the inspiration of Pope Innocent III, a name that will be forever associated with papal power and prestige. He is widely considered to be the greatest of the medieval Popes; and while I would agree with the powerful part, I have a fundamental issue with the man who claims to be God's representative on Earth instigating not one but two of the most brutal chapters in crusading history.

Less than ten years after Richard the Lionheart set sail from the Holy Land, Innocent III was calling for yet another crusade to the East. The plan for the Fourth Crusade was a smart one. While it was implied that Jerusalem would be the target (and it was the easiest destination to rally support), the actual plan was to attack Egypt. Egypt had been identified as the epicentre of Muslim power in the Middle East for decades. It was ironic that only a year after Richard left the Holy Land, Saladin died, casting his empire into turmoil. Therefore, as a new century dawned, why not use this chaos to the advantage of Christians and attack the key power base? This would relieve much of the pressure on the Christian lands on the east coast of the Mediterranean and could be used as a springboard for a successful campaign to Jerusalem.

It was an excellent strategy, further supported by the sensible suggestion that, since Richard had shown the benefits of shipping troops to the Holy Land, the next crusade should also be an amphibious undertaking (besides, a march around the Mediterranean basin to Egypt would be even longer than the one to Jerusalem).

A delegation was sent to Venice to discuss the building of a fleet. Numbers of troops were estimated, fleet size was calculated, indemnities were negotiated and deadlines were set. This crusade felt more like a business plan than the ramshackle but enthusiastic endeavours of the past. What could go wrong?

The undertaking was a huge deal for Venice. The resources it demanded meant that virtually all other business was put on hold while the colossal fleet was built and manned. Meanwhile, the preaching of the crusade was pushed forward by the powerhouse preacher that was Boniface of Montferrat. However, with the German empire tied up in one of its regular bouts of internal feuding, and England and France in open war, no kings were coming on this crusade. The situation also meant that a significant number of Europe's elite knights were otherwise engaged. So Boniface stirred up interest with noble families, and groups of crusaders started mustering.

The problem was that not enough troops were mustering. It became obvious fairly early on that the crusade was going to miss its estimated size by a considerable margin, so they postponed the deadline, hoping for a last-minute rush of enthusiasm. The rush was more of a dribble, so the crusade was in crisis before it had even started. The crusaders already assembled in Venice needed to be fed, and that meant yet more expense for the city, on top of the fact that the Venetians were clearly not going to be paid for a significant amount of the fleet they had built. The atmosphere grew tense. Innocent III wanted the crusade to get underway, while Venice wanted payment for the costs already incurred and agreed on in their contracts.

Consequently, a terrible and unsanctioned compromise was reached. Seeing that Venice had a fleet and an army at its disposal, why not use them to recover its losses in another way? The crusaders didn't like it, not one little bit. They had joined up to save Jerusalem (being oblivious to the fact that this was never the primary target); they did not want to become the mercenaries of the Republic of Venice. But the Doge (the elected leader of Venice), Enrico Dandolo, a blind old man in his nineties, was as shrewd as they come, and he had an idea.

The city of Zara (now Zadar) on the Dalmatian coast of Croatia had been an important Venetian trading post but had rebelled twenty years earlier. It was geographically close, Venice had a rightful claim to it and now had the muscle to do something about it. If the crusade was willing to capture Zara (a Christian city allied to the King of Hungary), the debt would be paid. While Richard the Lionheart's attack on Cyprus had been unintentional and the result of local hostility, the very point of a crusade was to fight against unbelievers, not believers. The proposal presented a terrible conundrum, and many of the crusaders left in disgust (including Simon de Montfort – more on him later). But after all was said and done, this one act would allow the crusade to continue on to Egypt, where it would do some 'real good'. Dandolo sweetened the deal with offers of Venetian assistance in the crusade proper.

The alternative was to go home with nothing; Jerusalem would be no closer to salvation. On a personal note, crusading oaths, while not exactly broken, certainly would not have been fulfilled and that guaranteed place in heaven not yet won. While many did go home, far more stayed and reluctantly agreed to the deal. From this point onwards, the Fourth Crusade was different from the previous ones. Once the deal had been struck, the crusade was no longer its own entity but a mercenary army for Venice. It may have been wrapped up in a different way and the chronicles may go to great lengths to show the reluctance of the crusaders, but fundamentally the crusaders were paying off a debt to Venice by doing what the Venetians (rather than the Pope) wanted.

On hearing of this, Innocent sent a letter threatening excommunication of the crusade, a first in crusading history and something of an oxymoron. After all, how could an army fighting for God not be doing the will of God? The papal letter was ignored, and the crusade set sail. Destination? Zara.

The siege of Zara in November 1202 was short, messy and an event that nobody seemed to want except for the Venetians. The people of Zara made the pointed reference that they, too, were Christians and obedient to the Pope by hanging banners marked with crosses from their windows and the city walls. There was a sense of anguish in the crusader camp. Putting it simply, this was not what they had signed up for. The siege lasted barely two weeks. The citizens of Zara had known the crusade was coming, but they couldn't resist an entire army, and the King of Hungary didn't send relief forces (he had taken a vow to go on this crusade, so he couldn't win, no matter what he did). Once inside, frustrations boiled over into extensive pillaging, and both the Venetians and the other crusaders clashed over the division of spoils.

To make matters worse, Innocent sent another letter, this time formally excommunicating all who were involved in the siege. Men went on crusade to receive God's blessing, not his wrath. This one document undermined everything, and had it become general knowledge it would have guaranteed the siege of Zara was the one and only act of the Fourth Crusade before it ended in ignominy. So the leaders of the crusade took the unprecedented step of ignoring the Pope, deciding also not to tell their followers about any of this. Fortunately for the leaders, their deception was covered by the very man they were ignoring, as Innocent shortly afterwards reconsidered his decision and retracted the excommunication.

The entire situation was a sorry mess, and it was now late in the campaigning season. The crusade decided it was best to winter at Zara, even though it felt like loitering at the scene of a crime. As the saying goes, 'if you don't ask, you don't get', and the Venetians had what they wanted. Now that they had gained one prize, maybe they could tempt the crusade with an even bigger one.

During the winter months, the youngest son of Frederick Barbarossa presented to the crusaders and Venetians the Byzantine prince Alexios IV Angelos, the son of the recently deposed Byzantine Emperor Isaac II Angelos. Alexios had a proposal. He assured the crusade that he was the rightful claimant to the throne, and claimed that if the crusade would travel with him to Constantinople, the gates would be flung open by joyous crowds, he would be crowned emperor and in return he would give troops, supplies and money as thanks to the crusaders. As a further inducement, he promised to heal the centuries-old schism between the Eastern and Western Churches and submit to papal authority. It was virtually a wish list come true. The crusade did need more men, and to heal the rift between brother Churches could only be a good thing, especially in the face of Islamic expansion. A trip to Constantinople, one of the most fabulous and famous cities in the world (with a population of about half a million, compared to London's then estimated 20,000), was on offer. What's not to love?

The simmering resentments between the Venetians and the other crusaders were quickly patched up. From the Venetian point of view, there were further benefits. Constantinople was the hub of trade from the East into the West. To help in this endeavour would allow them to get the very best trading terms with Byzantium, which would put them ahead of their Genoese rivals. This time Innocent was less hasty than after Zara; he was uneasy about the project (as were some of the crusaders), but he too would benefit if the plan worked. He didn't bless the endeavour, but he didn't condemn it, either.

So the crusade set sail, heading east rather than south. They arrived in the spring of 1203 with Alexios at their head, but his claim to the throne was greeted with bemusement. The Byzantines had an emperor, the uncle of Alexios, and they didn't need another one. The walls of the city had not been breached since they were built nearly 900 years earlier, and they had withstood larger armies than the force that surveyed them now.

Saying that, when a scouting force of eighty Frankish knights met a force of 500 Byzantine soldiers, the knights won, showing that the crusaders shouldn't be underestimated. Nevertheless, this plainly was not the reception the crusaders had anticipated. Once again, they were meant to undertake another assault of another Christian city; meanwhile, they remained a long way from their original goal. This crusade was going from bad to worse.

The First Crusade was triggered by a request for help from Byzantium. However, those events had unfolded against the backdrop of a split between the Eastern Orthodox Church and the Western papacy that had occurred a generation earlier. Ever since the Church had become part of the Roman Empire, there were rivalries between the Church leaders, but from the late seventh century onwards, many of the key patriarchs (Church leaders) were based in lands under Muslim rule. Jerusalem may have been the true seat of Christianity, but it had been one of the first to fall (almost irrevocably) under Muslim sway. By the time of the Fourth Crusade, the only remaining Christian power bases of any significant power were those in Constantinople and Rome – and they bickered constantly over which one had supremacy.

On some occasions, because of political rather than theological realities, one side would hold the advantage; but this never lasted. Then, in 1054, Cardinal Humbert of Moyenmoutier (from Rome) burst into Hagia Sophia (the Eastern Orthodox cathedral in Constantinople), walked up to the high altar mid-sermon, and formally excommunicated the Patriarch of Constantinople – and therefore the entire Eastern Church. It doesn't matter that he had no authority to do so, and it doesn't matter that at the time everyone thought it was one of the usual spats that would be resolved in due course. The reality was that more than 150 years later, the Eastern Church had yet to forgive and forget.

While the First Crusade had shown that these two hostile spheres of influence, if required, could work together, tensions were never far away. It's a sign of the unease between the two that by 1200, when Western Christians from the Crusades had forced entry into Orthodox churches, the local clergy felt the need to reconsecrate them, as if they had been desecrated by heathens rather than fellow Christians. The opportunity to heal the rift once and for all, particularly with the ever-present threat of Muslim powers to the east, should have benefitted everyone. As it was, however, the Fourth Crusade was a hostile force outside the imposing walls of Constantinople, supporting the claim of an emperor it didn't seem to want.

What should they do? Indeed, what *could* they do? After a discussion among the leaders, including, of course, the ever-present Enrico Dandolo, the decision for an assault was made. The plan was for the main crusader body to attack the land walls, while the Venetians would assault the sea walls of the Golden Horn. The Venetians pushed forward under a hail of missiles, took a section of the wall and captured two dozen towers. In the meantime, the rest of the crusade was stopped in its tracks by the Varangian Guard, the emperor's elite bodyguard. Clad head to foot in mail armour and wielding huge battle axes, they were fierce and fanatical in resistance. Backed up by the intimidating defences of the capital city itself, it was unsurprising the crusaders were getting nowhere fast.

With the land assault neutralised, the Varangian Guard was able to move down the lines and meet the Venetian soldiers on the wall. Again the attackers were no match for such exemplary soldiers, so the Venetians started a fire to create confusion and then beat a hasty retreat.

The plan worked. In all the smoke, heat and chaos, the Venetians were able to successfully disengage from the assault and head back to their ships. The makeshift plan for withdrawal had kept the bulk of the crusader forces intact. But the plan produced unintended consequences when the fire at the walls spread to nearby wooden houses, and the flames quickly tuned into an inferno, an unstoppable wall of roaring fury.

Fire finally stirred the dithering Emperor Alexios III, who brought forward the rest of his army and marched out towards the crusaders. Alexios had the people behind him as they watched in horror while parts of their beautiful city were engulfed in flames. The crusaders were outnumbered and tired after a gruelling assault. Now was the time to attack.

Except that he didn't. For some unknown reason, he

panicked and returned to the city without even an exchange of angry words. This clearly was not what the situation required, and the usually sycophantic (at least to an emperor's face) court rose up in disgust, demanding that Alexios III act like an emperor and take action! Alexios calmed them and claimed he would fight; but that night, taking one of his daughters along with the crown jewels, he fled to Thrace. This completely hopeless and cowardly ruler left behind his wife and other daughters to fend for themselves.

The reasons for Alexios's failures are unclear. To abandon an impregnable capital city and to refuse to fight after raising an army at a time of national crisis was political suicide. Quite why Alexios III imploded so spectacularly we'll never know; but now, with an enemy army camped beneath the capital's walls, the citizens of Byzantium, with no leader, were dangerously vulnerable.

Once Alexios III's cowardly flight was discovered, the courtiers quickly released the blind old emperor (Isaac II, the father of Alexios IV) and gave him back his palace, along with everything else. Best not to anger the new management, even if it just so happened that it had been badly treated by the old management.

Meanwhile, the crusade was in a state of confusion. The crusaders had been close to taking the city. They would have been able to see the plumes of dark smoke, showing part of the city to be on fire. They had seen the emperor march through the gates with an army easily large enough to crush them, and then, inexplicably, march back into the city without a fight. It must have left them scratching their heads.

Then, the very next day, the gates were flung open and Isaac II, now looking very much like an emperor, dressed as he was in imperial splendour, went out of the city to greet his son and welcome in the crusaders. Maybe things were finally looking up for this blighted endeavour.

There was, of course, the small matter of a raging fire. It lasted for three days before it was brought under control, partly dying out of its own accord. When the smoke had cleared, the citizens were shocked to see that some 400 acres of their city were now ash and charcoal. About 20,000 people were left homeless.

Alexios IV had offered huge incentives to the crusaders to get them to come to Constantinople, and they had fulfilled their side of the bargain; he was now joint emperor with his father. The problem was that making a commitment and fulfilling one are not the same thing.

Alexios IV is an interesting figure. He was a chancer who'd come to Zara to make a deal with a group who didn't want to have anything to do with him in order to gain one of the richest prizes in Europe. You have to admire that level of ambition. What happened after the capture of the city was not exactly his fault; but, undeniably, he did create some of the circumstances. The crusaders wanted payment, but Alexios III had just run off with most of the ready cash, so most of their money would have to come from taxes, tributes and levies, all of which took both time and stability to gather. In the meantime, there were thousands of Latin crusaders roaming around the city, looking for fun or trouble – one often leading to the other.

The people of Byzantium were hugely proud (some might say haughty). They believed that their culture and links to antiquity made them superior to most, and they referred to themselves as Romans, even though Greek had been the standard language for about 600 years. There was no way they could tolerate a foreign occupation of their capital. Nor would they allow a puppet emperor, dependent on Western power, to stay on the sacred throne. Worse still, the Orthodox Church was, in many ways, the foundation of their cultural identity; and now the people were being told that they must follow the Pope and all his 'heretical' teachings. A new leader needs a power base and time to succeed. Alexios IV had neither.

Grumbles turned to ominous rumblings, and these grew into full-scale riots. One of their leaders was the imperial chamberlain, the marvellously named Alexios Dukas Murtzurphlus (the last word literally means 'bushy eyebrows', so we can get an idea of what he looked like). He was a firebrand speaker and an inciter of constant anti-Latin (Western) feeling.

In January 1204, Isaac II died. Alexios IV knew this was the moment the crowds had been waiting for. As the mob attacked the Blachernae palace, Alexios naively asked Murtzurphlus to go to the crusaders and get help. But Murtzurphlus did no such thing. Meanwhile, with events moving very quickly, the Latins dithered. As chaos grew, the crusaders' decision was made for them when, at the end of January, Alexios IV was found strangled. With a real power vacuum and no obvious claimants to the throne, the rebel turned himself into emperor, and Murtzurphlus became Alexios V.

The Fourth Crusade had arrived at Constantinople to put Alexios IV on the throne and then had hung around mainly out of self-interest. Theoretically, the crusaders were there to help the new emperor. With Isaac and now Alexios IV dead, there was no reason why they should still be there. But after all their hard-earned gains and concessions, the crusade faced leaving Constantinople empty-handed. Allowing a vociferously anti-Western emperor to remain in charge of the city was not an option.

Emperor Alexios V wanted this alien army to move from his territory, but the crusaders hung on, saying that they had a signed treaty with the previous emperor that had yet to be honoured. The crusaders' argument was weak. Alexios V was never going to ratify a treaty that he had been rebelling against for nearly a year. But in the meantime, he was just as vulnerable as his predecessor and desperately needed time and funds to turn a palace coup into the start of a successful reign.

Very quickly, and very predictably, the relationship between the two interests broke down. The Venetians and the rest of the crusade agreed that it was time to put an end to this and carried out their own palace coup. If successful, the resulting Latin empire of Byzantium would be split between crusader and Venetian interests.

The events of April 1204 eerily mirrored the events of July 1203. The crusade assaulted by land and, thanks to the Venetians, by sea too. Again the Varangian Guard put up a furious defence. This time, when the Venetians started to waver, the blind old Doge demanded that his own galley be rowed into the fray, to shame the others to get back in the fight. It worked.

The crusaders were now breaching the walls on both sides, so the occupants, having learned nothing from the last assault, thought that setting fire to some of the houses would stop the attack. The first fire had been started by the Venetians; the second was started by the citizens of Constantinople. Just as before, an emperor was forced to swallow his pride and flee for his life, although Alexios V had put more effort into the defence of his city than the cowardly Alexios III.

The crusaders prevailed, but again, fire raged. By the time the second one had been put out, a further 15,000 people had lost their homes. But on this occasion, rather than showing restraint, the crusaders went on a rampage, sacking the city for three days (as was customary after the successful completion of a contested siege assault).

Baldwin of Flanders was chosen and agreed upon as the man who would become the first Latin emperor of the Byzantine Empire. He was crowned in Hagia Sophia as Baldwin I of Constantinople. Other vassal or Latin states were created, including the Kingdom of Thessalonica and the Venetian Duchy of the Archipelago. The Byzantines themselves were not out for the count. A number of satellite states with various claimants to the throne existed on the periphery of Latin power, the focal point being the Empire of Nicaea.

Many crusaders got rich from the lands gained from this endeavour, but it had been at a heavy cost to the image of crusading. There had been attacks on Christian sites before, and there were plenty in the West who were deeply suspicious of the decadent Byzantine Empire, but a crusade that never even got close to fighting Muslims, or even to reaching the Holy Land – can that really even be called a crusade? The clear-cut narrative of the official crusades is undeniably muddied from this point onwards.

A number of contemporaries in the West were aghast at the sacking of the largest city in Europe by crusaders. The stories of fires, massacres and looting hardly befitted even the thirteenth-century idea of acceptable behaviour on a crusade, the very purpose of which was to defend Christendom, not pillage it.

Much of what we know about the crusade comes from the vivid first-hand account written by Geoffrey of Villehardouin. This French knight was part of the committee who agreed the original deal with Venice and was present throughout all the traumas that followed. Although biased, even he recognised the dubious nature of the crusaders' actions. The reality was that the Fourth Crusade did not end with the sacking of Constantinople. In fact, Villehardouin continues with his account of a number of other campaigns. In order to solidify its borders against aggressive and hostile neighbours, years of hard fighting were still to come.

However, for the time being, the crusading movement had a new ally in the Near East, and one that would be far easier to deal with than the old regime. Innocent III was now able to claim the unification of the two Churches and dominance over the Patriarch of Constantinople. Enrico Dandolo, at a time when most men of his age were either dying or just happy to be in a comfy bed, had been on crusade, greatly increasing the position and the power of Venice. His other gift to Venice was the bronze statues from the Hippodrome of Constantinople. More than 800 years later, they are known as 'the Horses of St Mark' and are still installed in St Mark's Square, at the very centre of Venice. They are a constant reminder of the plunder stolen by the Fourth Crusade.

6

Heresy: The Albigensian Crusade in France

Even as the Fourth Crusade continued to subdue its unruly subjects and clash with hostile neighbours, other developments were taking place in the very core of Europe. Before the dust had settled from the previous crusade, these were to trigger the next one.

In the history of the papacy, many popes called for a crusade – and a number had done it more than once – but only Innocent III managed to launch two crusades that amounted to anything (there were other plans, too – more on those later).

But first, another little bit of Church history. In Europe the idea of a heretic is well known. There is the official religious line, and anyone who does not agree with that is condemned as an unbeliever, with the presumption being that only Hell awaits after death. However, the further east you go, the more the notion of 'the heretic' fades. It's a concept that doesn't really work in Hinduism or Buddhism, in which individuals are allowed to have a different take on teachings.

'The heretic' is a Western invention, and the organisation that did more than any other of the Western Churches to entrench doctrinal compliance was the Church based in Rome. And rather embarrassingly for that Church, it was losing its authority in southern France. This area was often referred to as the Languedoc and was at the geographical centre of Western Christianity. Quite simply, the Church could not allow any deviation from its official interpretation of scripture, and it was alarmed by events so close to home. This heresy was an unforgivable challenge to its authority.

This divergent religious view has come to be known as the Cathar heresy. Cathars believed in the Bible, but took a different view on Heaven and Hell. Cathars believed that the physical world was blatantly corrupt, as evidenced by disease, war, famine, suffering, inequality and death. Are these not all the work of the Devil? So they came to the (not illogical) conclusion that the physical world was created by the Devil. This world was something to be endured until a beautiful release into the afterlife, which was perfect and the place of God.

If you start playing around with this theory it can sound alluring, but it does lead to some interesting conclusions. If the physical world is bad, then reproduction should be discouraged. The Cathars believed that a happy soul floated around until rudely ensnared into the fleshy prison that is a baby. That soul will now have a life on Earth in which to prove itself worthy enough to get back to Paradise. And if that doesn't make you feel guilty as a parent, nothing will.

Ironically, while their concepts should have led to a dwindling of population and a natural fading out of the sect, it was in rude health by the start of the thirteenth century. And it was not at all secretive. The Cathars had their own churches, bishops and counter organisation to the Roman Catholic Church. Even some of the nobles of southern France were Cathars. Heretic and Roman Catholic lived side by side, with no more friction than would normally be expected in a town.

This relative peace was shattered in 1207, when Raymond, Count of Toulouse, was excommunicated by Innocent III. An interdict was placed on his lands; and in essence, there was a papal demand for civil disobedience against him. It turned out that Raymond was more popular with the local population than the Pope was, and the Pope's orders were widely ignored. Innocent realised he was going to get nowhere with his current attitude, so Raymond was reconciled with the Church. However, in 1208 a crowd of angry locals descended on a Roman church where the Papal Legate, Pierre de Castelnau, was murdered. Pierre had been trying to preach to the local Cathars to get them back into the Roman flock and so became a symbol of papal interference in the Languedoc.

Raymond was again blamed, and this time the excommunication stuck. But to make matters worse, in this case, the blood of a priest had been drawn and that was a step too far. Church historians talk about the marvel of Innocent III's authority and his ability to organise two crusades, and this is correct. But unlike many medieval and Renaissance popes, he was also a devout Christian. He displayed no decadence, had no mistresses and led a blameless personal life.

It is also worth remembering that the results of the Fourth Crusade were a long way from the original plan envisioned by Innocent. He had been personally so appalled by the crusade's journey to Zara that he had even (albeit briefly) excommunicated the entire crusade. However, he also had witnessed how one good plan had become a botched job, leading to terrifyingly destructive consequences. Innocent III should have learnt that starting a war is easy, but that it is the unexpected consequences of such an undertaking that should make one wary. The sacking of Constantinople may have had its advantages for the papacy, but it was an embarrassment. Innocent had blood on his hands.

But he did not learn from the campaign in Byzantium. Instead, he intended to use the blunt instrument of crusade to resolve the delicate crisis in southern France.

This new crusade was to become known not as the Fifth Crusade but as the Albigensian Crusade, named after the town of Albi, a centre of the Cathar heresy and the scene of heavy fighting. Innocent III clearly had learnt nothing from the Fourth Crusade because the levels of cruelty and barbarity actually rose during this latest crusader cause. With the multiple massacres that ensued, there were few cries of concern from the papacy, a colossal black mark against Innocent III's reputation. Even worse for all involved, this was easily the longest crusade, lasting a full twenty years, a timeline which meant that Innocent never got to see the outcome of his plan. In fact, for all his crusader fervour, Innocent never actually saw any of his main crusades fight Muslims.

Philip Augustus, who had been a major participant in the Third Crusade, had by 1208 seen Richard the Lionheart die in a freak accident and had subdued the new English king, John, in the north of France. So he took this opportunity to work with the Pope to reinforce his authority in the south. While France was one of the most ancient kingdoms in Europe, it was rarely unified as a single entity under the king for any length of time during the medieval era. By comparison, the King of England might face the occasional revolt, but through the centuries, English monarchs enjoyed far more authority over the entirety of England than most French kings did over France.

So the French king (and other northern subjects, including Anglo-Norman nobles) marched south. The main problem became apparent very quickly: how can you tell the difference between a heretic and non-heretic in France? At least in the Middle East, those that didn't look European could be deemed to be the enemy (even though that lumps together Muslims, Jews and varieties of Eastern Christian).

In 1209 the crusaders arrived at the fortified town of Béziers, led by the Papal Legate, Arnaud-Amaury, Abbot of

Cîteaux. When they arrived, they sent a message ordering the townsfolk to expel all the heretics; the crusade would deal with them and leave the town in peace. Of course, the Cathars were not a separate community, and family members were not going to betray each other on the order of interlopers from the north. Béziers was a microcosm of another major problem for the Albigensian Crusade: the people of the Languedoc were more loyal to each other than to external authorities. The Pope might well see this as a clear-cut way of removing heresy, but the men doing the fighting saw this as imposing northern French dominance on the south. The people of Béziers (and elsewhere) would do everything to resist this, even if it meant 'good' Christians fighting alongside so-called heretics.

While the crusaders began to set up camp and settle in for a siege, there was an attempt by the men of Béziers to attack the crusade, leaving it in disarray. A small town fighting against veteran soldiers could only lead to one end: instead of besieging Béziers, the attack was quickly repulsed and the crusaders pushed through the gates and into the town. A cry went up, asking how they could tell the difference between heretics and good Catholics. Arnaud-Amaury replied, 'Kill them all for the Lord shall know his own.' What happened next was a full-scale massacre; the crusaders butchered anyone they could find. The main (Catholic) church was burned down, and non-heretic priests were murdered as they sought refuge next to their own altars.

In Arnaud-Amaury's own words:

> Our men spared no one, irrespective of rank, sex or age, and put to the sword almost 20,000 people. After this great slaughter the whole city was despoiled and burnt.

The numbers are (thankfully) exaggerated, but it is chilling to read such an unapologetic statement from an abbot, supposedly a man of peace. But the situation does show a certain medieval logic: if a good Christian died by violent means, then he became a martyr. By that thought process, the butchery at Béziers was a theologically sound way of sorting the Christians from the heretics, as God would be doing his infallible sorting in the afterlife. Of course, by the same logic, burning down churches and murdering good Christians would mean that the crusaders themselves were now condemned to damnation, but that didn't seem to occur to Arnaud-Amaury.

With Béziers a charnel house of smouldering ruins, the crusade marched on, knowing that their bloody reputation preceded them. They then came to the walled city of Carcassonne (the inspiration for the board game), which in theory stood a good chance of resisting a siege. Unfortunately, refugees in the area, after hearing of the Béziers massacre, had flocked to the town, which was now overpopulated, a perilous situation with the prospect of a long siege and too many mouths to feed.

Within a week of the crusaders' arrival, the town's water supply had been diverted; and even though he had come to the crusader camp under a flag of truce, the town's spokesperson was taken prisoner. By comparison with Béziers, the deal offered this time was generous. Everyone was to strip naked and leave the town (some dispute that this was literally meant and think it was really intended that they should wear underwear, but I think it should be taken as stated since the point was humiliation). The townsfolk knew a good deal when they heard one and trudged out of the city under the watchful eyes of the crusaders.

At this point Simon de Montfort (this was the father of the other Simon de Montfort, who fought Henry III of England) became the de facto head of the crusade, and more towns fell in 1209 and 1210. Investing in siege after siege was a slow business, which explains why it took so long to get to the largest Cathar town, Toulouse. The nature of France was that there was always a walled town or castle to capture if an army intended to properly hold an area.

Because it had taken the crusade more than two years to reach Toulouse, Raymond had had more than adequate time to anticipate the siege. The year 1211 marks the point where, for the first time, the crusaders failed to capture the town before them and were forced to retreat.

Let's pause there and get a quick update on the situation south of the border in Spain. At the same time that the Albigensian Crusade was bogging down around Toulouse, the Almohad Caliphate in Spain was turning the tide against the Christian kingdoms of the Iberian Peninsula. For fifteen years the Almohads had been pushing back the Christians; but in 1211, Muhammad al-Nasir invaded Christian territory and captured the stronghold of Salvatierra. This was the trigger for Innocent III to … go on, guess. Yes, that's right – call a crusade! He was really getting the hang of it now. The subsequent campaign was also not considered to be the Fifth Crusade; although as you can see by now, the numbering of crusades was a little arbitrary.

The army that assembled in 1212 was a multinational and polyglot force that included the Knights Templar. They had received papal indulgences for the remission of sins in return for going on crusade, so they were strapping on their armour to fight Muslims (a first for Innocent III). It was a crusade by any other name and shows how the dynastic desires of the Iberian Christian princes had now blurred irretrievably with the crusader cause.

The climax of this campaign was the Battle of Las Navas de Tolosa. The Christian army was led by the three monarchs of Christian Spain and Portugal, Sancho VII of Navarre, Alfonso VIII of Castile and Peter II of Aragon. It was Alfonso who was the overall leader, and the Christian army was huge by the standards of European armies, about

50,000 strong. However, Muhammad al-Nasir had an army about four times the size, and its camp was protected by mountains.

The Iberian princes got local Christians to guide the crusader army through rarely used mountain paths, which allowed the army to completely surprise and outmanoeuvre the Almohads. The result was one of the most important and decisive battles in European history, unfortunately now mostly forgotten everywhere but Spain. The Christians fell on the unprepared Almohad camp and cut through it like a hot knife through butter. Muhammad al-Nasir only escaped by having thousands of slave soldiers chained around his personal tent (he died only a few months later in Marrakesh). By the end of the day, more than 100,000 Muslims had been killed or captured, with losses of less than 10 per cent for the crusaders.

From the Christian point of view, this was a miracle; as a symbol of this divine blessing, Muhammad al-Nasir's tent and standard were sent to Innocent III. The legacy of this battle cannot be exaggerated. At the time the Christian opportunity to proceed further south into Iberia had faded and, if anything, was more likely to be facing further reversals. After the Battle of Las Navas de Tolosa, the various Muslim dynasties of Iberia never again gained the upper hand or the initiative. It is only after 1211 that it is possible to begin to talk about the slow death of Islamic influence in Spain; even then, it would take more than 250 years to oust the last Muslim prince from Grenada. Sancho VII of Navarre adopted a new coat of arms to celebrate his achievements at the battle: golden chains on a red background (a reminder of the slaves chained to the tent), which is incorporated into the Spanish flag of today. That's how important this battle is in Spain.

Sancho, Alfonso and Peter had stopped the Almohad juggernaut and become heroes in the eyes of the Christian orld. Their futures would be mixed, but they all recognised ...e strategic advantages this victory had secured them.

So as success met success in Spain, the Albigensian Crusade ground on. The main reason for its length was the fact that often, after the crusader force left a town, it would rise up in revolt. Nobody could justify the constant massacring of populations; most of the atrocities happened in the first few years of the war and tailed off during the coming twenty years. However, there was one occasion where an entire town was blinded and then required to march along as a winding column of stumbling vagrants, each person putting a hand on the shoulder of the person in front, while the man at the head of the column was left with one eye to guide this wretched host. Once again, Innocent III's 'simple' plan led to cruelty piled on cruelty.

But the atrocities weren't just on the crusaders' side. Violence breeds violence and a number of monks, abbots and bishops were murdered simply because of their beliefs. It was quite common for the defenders of cities to mutilate the corpses of any crusader they could get their hands on. Then there's Elise de Cazenac, a Cathar who carried out a number of atrocities in the Dordogne area. On one occasion, she ordered the mutilation of 150 townsfolk. They had their hands and legs cut off and all were blinded.

In 1213 Simon de Montfort again threatened to lay siege to Toulouse, so Raymond asked for help from anywhere he could get it, including his brother-in-law, Peter II of Aragon, one of the heroes of the Battle of Las Navas de Tolosa. This request shows how complicated the situation had become in southern France. Raymond had been excommunicated and was now defending heretics in direct contradiction to the wishes of the Pope. Peter, by contrast, had just been on crusade and was a poster boy of the crusading ideal. However, Peter obviously thought that blood was thicker than water (or religion) and joined Raymond in defence of the Languedoc against Simon de Montfort and the Albigensian Crusade.

The result was the Battle of Muret. Raymond and Peter had managed to muster a force of approximately 25,000 from their own forces and other towns, including Carcassonne (which had been captured by the crusade and underlined the serious problems the crusade faced in trying to impose any real long-term influence in the area).

In 1213 Muret was a small town very near Toulouse that had recently fallen to the crusade. So Peter arrived just in time to try and recapture it. Part of the army immediately began assaulting the walls, using its advantages in numbers to present several targets for Simon de Montfort. Although Peter and Raymond's army was split, each section was larger than Simon's force of only 1,500 men.

However, what Simon lacked in numbers he made up for in experience and quality, because his force was the cream of his army. It was well armed, and all the men were wearing full mail armour and helm.

Peter was no fool and did not underestimate his foe, so he anchored his army to a river on one side and to a marsh area on the other; this would stop Simon's heavy cavalry from trying to outflank him. Simon split his forces into three independent and self-sufficient units and issued the simplest of orders – charge!

Peter was used to fighting the more mobile and lighter-armoured Muslim horse archers of the Almohads and may not ever have been on the receiving end of a direct attack by the northern European heavy cavalry. But Raymond had and he suggested to Peter that the best course of action would be to break up the charge with archers, a sound tactic under the circumstances. However, Peter declined, feeling that such an action would be unchivalrous. Peter then put on armour with no royal insignia and joined the front line to face combat.

The sledgehammer of the crusader cavalry fell on the Aragonese soldiers, smashing into their front ranks, right where Peter was. He was one of the first to die. A king was a highly prized captive, worth a huge ransom, so had he been wearing his full livery, his life surely would have been saved; but as he was clad in nondescript armour, he was one of the first to fall. At this point, with their king dead, the army disintegrated. The battle had echoes of the Battle of Las Navas de Tolosa, where a tiny force of crusaders shattered a huge enemy army. It was just a shame for Peter that he happened to be on the receiving end this time around. Raymond was forced to flee, and Muret remained in crusader hands.

It would take Simon another three years to finally capture Toulouse and proclaim himself count; but less than a year later, when Simon went off campaigning again, the city revolted and reinstated Raymond. It was also about this time that Innocent III ended all of the indulgences connected with the crusade. As he no longer had any spiritual reason to continue conquering, Simon felt cut adrift. It was all starting to look more grubby than holy. The crusade was in danger of stalling, but with Toulouse in revolt, Innocent had no option but to reinstate these indulgences, which gave Simon all the legitimacy he needed. These actions show that while the campaigning associated with the Albigensian Crusade lasted twenty years, the actual time a crusader needed to fight in order to acquire an indulgence was neither consistent nor automatically granted. In 1217 Simon returned to Toulouse to retake the city, even if it killed him.

Despite previous orders to destroy the defences of Toulouse, he returned with a crusader army to discover they were intact. Inside the town, the defenders had been busy building their own trebuchets to fire on any advancing siege weapons the crusaders might produce. A trebuchet was the height of medieval siege technology and the most powerful artillery invented before gunpowder. The kinetic energy produced by one of these machines could hurl large boulders up to half a mile, taking out huge chunks of defensive wall, all from a safe distance.

The siege ground on until June 1218, when the crusaders tried yet another assault, this time with a covered shelter called a 'cat'. This was disabled, and later the defenders left their positions to destroy it once and for all. A skirmish broke out around the cat as the crusaders tried to preserve it and the defenders tried to burn it to the ground. When Simon de Montfort's brother was wounded by a crossbow bolt through his leg, Simon went to his aid. It was at this point that Simon was crushed by a rock, hurled from a trebuchet operated by women and children. The great crusader warrior had been slain by girls and boys, and the destruction caused by a direct trebuchet hit (a very rare occurrence on a battlefield) probably meant they had only pieces to pick up.

With the death of their leader, the crusaders quickly lost interest, and the third siege of Toulouse resulted in victory for Raymond. While Simon de Montfort had perished in 1218, Innocent III died in 1216; now two of the chief instigators of the crusade were gone. There followed a period of stagnation. Had the crusade ended here, it could have been considered, in every sense, a failure. The result of ten years of fighting was multiple massacres and no change to the status quo of the Languedoc's political and religious practices. Some cities (most notably Carcassonne) had eventually become crusader enclaves, but the outpouring of blood and treasure for such gains had clearly not been worth it.

The second stage of the Albigensian Crusade ignited with the sons of most of the key players. In 1224 Simon de Montfort's son, Amalric, claimed the territories of his father in the Languedoc area. This was supported by Philip

Augustus's son, Louis VIII; and in 1225, Raymond of Toulouse's son (another Raymond) managed to get himself excommunicated by Pope Honorius III.

As sheer brute force had clearly resulted in rather muted success, there was a determined increase in another, much newer weapon in the Church's armoury. Today it is called the Congregation for the Doctrine of the Faith, but it will be forever known as the Inquisition.

The Inquisition came about in the late twelfth century for the specific purpose of rooting out heresy, and it was the Cathar heresy that enabled the refinement of its methods. It was to be so effective in its ability to eliminate those ideologically opposed to the Church's central authority that its practices have been mimicked in a number of totalitarian regimes.

Contrary to popular belief, brutal torture and executions were rare. The first Inquisition was temporarily established in Languedoc in 1184. However, after the failure of the initial stages of the Albigensian Crusade, it was permanently established in Carcassonne in 1229. The Inquisitors were either Dominican or Franciscan Friars; unlike monks, these holy men were used to travelling around and preaching. However, during the Inquisition, instead of preaching, they held religious courts. The more physical aspects, such as incarceration, torture or execution, were carried out by local civil (non-religious) authorities.

The court would be set up in a town where people were brought before it on the grounds of heresy, or some other crime against the Church (as opposed to a civil crime). They had an opportunity to explain themselves, but if there were other confessions or contradictory statements from associates or neighbours, the person was considered to be guilty anyway. They would then face a maximum penalty, which might not be death but could be the forfeit of goods, and/or excommunication ... unless ... and it's that 'unless' which has been used by many religious and totalitarian courts since ...

... Unless the accused had information about other heretics. Now the web of heresy could be unpicked. That was the theory, of course, but the reality was that the motivation was the very human feeling of revenge: if I'm going down, I'm going to take a few people with me. So, completely innocent people were often accused because of a long-held grudge against them. Pretty soon most of a town would be guilty of heresy, irrespective of how accurate the findings actually were.

Now, with so many people guilty of various ecclesiastical crimes, fines could be implemented, property could be seized, and on some occasions people would be executed. It was a very dubious business. Torture wasn't a regular feature, but incarceration until confession was. Imagine being locked up for a crime you didn't commit, knowing the only way to get to trial was by confessing to the crime.

I am no apologist for the Inquisition, and while the death count and lurid stories of torture are exaggerated, the reality isn't much better. Here we have holy men, who were supposed to have an understanding of the New Testament, dishing out Old Testament punishment in a way that Jesus almost certainly would not have endorsed. Some have argued that kings did worse to traitors or rebels, and on this there can be no argument; but the Church had gone from being an institution of spiritual knowledge and teaching to being one of predators in search of theological free-thinkers in order to eradicate them. It's hard to call it anything other than a corruption of the original values of Jesus. While it is true that the friars never conducted any of the torture or executions, it's a fine line between carrying out the act and allowing it to take place. The executioners were, after all, 'only following orders' – an excuse used many times with often chilling outcomes.

Imagine the sheer terror that accompanied the announcement that an Inquisitor had arrived in town. Were you safe? Whom had you wronged? Were they above reproach? Would it be better to run and leave your hard-won property and belongings behind? If you did that, you would certainly be guilty, in which case would you be condemning the rest of your family. It was guilt by association. Even if you were one of the lucky ones who managed to avoid condemnation or to escape with a minor fine, the whole process would have been truly nerve shredding. And after the Inquisition had left, the local balance of power would definitely have changed. Long-established families could be broken, while some new faces inherited the property of heretics.

That heretics were burned at the stake was the result of contemporary theological logic. The idea was that the burning process might help their souls rise to heaven. Similarly, confession before burning meant a quick garrotting, a merciful release rather than a slow and agonising death at the stake. This was not a trick to gain confessions; once tied to those bundles of wood, everyone knew it could only end one way. The question was: would your death be quick or slow? A quick confession and it could all be over … better than being roasted alive.

Like the Crusades, the Inquisition was a medieval invention. They were intertwined as tools (weapons) the papacy could use against the two-headed monster of heresy and Islam. Neither of these tools formally existed before the 1090s; and yet by the mid-thirteenth century they were both commonplace in European society.

The Inquisition was to play several key roles in the history of the Crusades, and its usefulness in protecting Church doctrine saw the concept evolve rather than dissipate. And it exists to this day (Pope Benedict XVI was in charge of this office before being elected Pope in 2005). The Congregation for the Doctrine of the Faith no longer burns people who disagree with it, but a practising Catholic doesn't want to get on its bad side, either.

So the second phase of the Albigensian Crusade comprised the two-pronged assault of military muscle, along with the Inquisition, which scoured the newly conquered areas for any potential members of a fifth column. It was exactly what was needed. Using another modern parallel, the Albigensian Crusade had attempted the occupation of a hostile territory with traditional forces, allowing the rise of a continuous insurgency. The Inquisition acted as a highly effective anti-insurgency force. Now the Cathars had nowhere to hide.

The trigger for the second phase of concentrated military action came in November 1225, when Raymond of Toulouse (son of the other Raymond) was excommunicated – like father, like son. A Church council then authorised a tax on the French Church. It was a tithe charged against annual incomes and became known as the 'Albigensian tenth'. This tax was designed to pay for a French problem with French money and is another sign that the international nature of the Crusades was on the wane.

But the monies raised were not enough and had to be bolstered by the finances and leadership of the French king, Louis VIII. In June 1226 he marched his army of northerners into the Languedoc, where many towns and forts quickly surrendered. The crusade had its tactics in order; it was well funded and led by a king – and the Inquisition was also stalking the area.

But Avignon resisted. It was well defended and could count on support from Frederick II, the German Emperor, who nominally had rights to the city. Louis's siege commenced, but as weeks turned to months it dawned on the defenders that a German relief army was not coming. Best to strike a deal before Louis breached the walls, which would entitle him to sack the city, according to the code of conduct at the time.

This delay was to yield an unexpected twist to events, which occurred just two months later when Louis died of dysentery. It looked for a moment as if the whole endeavour might end then and there. The heir to the throne, Louis IX, was just twelve years old, but the widowed queen, Blanche of Castile, allowed the crusade to continue under the supervision of Humbert de Beaujeu.

Humbert spent the next three years tenaciously grinding down the Languedoc. By 1229 they were back at Toulouse and this time they employed a scorched earth policy, destroying crops, cattle and even vineyards. Although this would devalue the city itself, it would also cripple any future resistance. This was to be the fourth and final siege of the city.

Unlike before, the Count of Toulouse didn't have any allies from beyond his borders, and the final city of Cathar resistance was surrounded. But a cornered animal can be dangerous, and Queen Blanche offered Raymond a way out that didn't involve a bloody last stand. A treaty was proposed which allowed Raymond to continue as the ruler of Toulouse in exchange for fighting Cathars, returning all Church property and destroying the formidable defences of Toulouse. In short he was told to back the winners, and in return all would be forgiven. Naturally, Raymond agreed to this generous offer and signed the Treaty of Paris in 1229.

To seal the deal, Raymond became part of the royal family when one of his daughters married one of Blanche's sons. There was one minor humiliation when he was briefly imprisoned and flogged, but it was a small price to pay to remain the Count of Toulouse, with a daughter who was now a Capetian princess.

So the Albigensian Crusade, the longest crusade, ended neither in a huge victory parade nor with buckets of blood in a vicious last stand. While the initial trigger may have been religious, it was, in reality, very much an exercise by the French monarchy to centralise its authority. This would be a long process and wouldn't truly finish until the mid-fifteenth century. In the meantime, though, the Cathar heresy was crushed and would be remembered mainly by conspiracy theorists and Church historians.

Meanwhile, the numbered crusades were getting on track again with a Muslim (rather than Christian) target. The Fifth Crusade occurred early on in the story of the Albigensian Crusade, but it's a story worth telling.

7

The Crusades Go to Egypt: The Fifth Crusade and the Changing Nature of the Crusading Movement

While Innocent III had put the wheels in motion for the Fifth Crusade, its delay was due to the other plans he had hatched. So the call for a Fifth Crusade came from Pope Honorius III. Looking at the main leaders of the crusade, it is possible to see the relationships that were building because of the all the crusading activity.

Andrew II of Hungary had been fighting in the Balkans, taking advantage of the shifting balance of power after the Fourth Crusade. He even married into the new Latin imperial line of Constantinople, but the Latin nobles had thwarted his attempts to become emperor. He had had to fight for his throne after his father's death and had allied with Leopold VI of Austria.

Leopold was from a new generation where crusading could be a full-time calling. He had already fought in Spain against the Almohads, had been on campaign in the Albigensian Crusade and was now to be one of the major players in the Fifth Crusade.

Louis VIII, King of France, would have gone on the crusade had he not been keen to finish with the Cathars in southern France. England was also otherwise occupied.

After the disastrous reign of King John, the country was picking up the pieces after a civil war and was now under the leadership of the boy king Henry III.

The only other dynasty to have form in the crusading movement was that of the German emperors. However, the current one (Frederick II, whose tutor had been Pope Honorius III himself) was forever falling out with the Pope; and as he had been excommunicated, he wasn't allowed to join, even though he wanted to.

The plan picked up where the Fourth Crusade had started. Everyone knew that it would be pointless to attack Jerusalem directly as the real power belonged to the Ayyubid dynasty in Egypt. The plan was therefore the same as the original one for the Fourth Crusade: neutralise Ayyubid power around Jerusalem before going for the prize itself.

A giant pincer movement was envisaged, with Andrew, the Latin Emperor of Constantinople, and the armies of the Holy Land fighting in Syria, while the other European forces were to land in Egypt. It was an ambitious, well-calculated plan; and as Pope Honorius had previously been the papal financial expert, the Venetians weren't going to get the upper hand this time. Also, with the resources of the new, Latin-run, Byzantine Empire being brought into play in the crusading movement, we can see a positive legacy of the Fourth Crusade. This new player created a boost to the military capacity of the crusade.

Andrew's campaign in 1217 brought together a huge crusader army for the first time in Outremer since the Third Crusade, more than twenty years earlier. As it neared Jerusalem the Ayyubid governor was forced to destroy the city's defences, enabling a potential recapture with ease; and with the Muslim population mindful of the bloodbaths of the First Crusade, many fled with their families and belongings.

Andrew and his forces were confronted by Saphadin, whose actual name was Al-Adil. The Frankish name Saphadin comes from the honorific title Sayf al-Din, which means 'sword of faith'. Al-Adil had been a major power in Syria since the time of Saladin. He was an effective governor, general and politician, preferring peace with the Crusader States, which allowed him to solidify his hold on other key Muslim towns and enabled his rule over a vast territory stretching from Syria to Egypt.

By the time this new threat arrived he was in his seventies, but he was determined to live up to his title and met Andrew and his forces near the River Jordan in November. The battle had none of the significance of Ascalon or Hattin, but it was a win for the crusade. Quite sensibly, Al-Adil moved his troops back behind the fortified walls of the various strongholds and cities under his authority. What happened next was a stalemate: Andrew's forces were too strong for Al-Adil to destroy, but the crusaders didn't have the time or siege equipment to capture fortresses such as the formidable Mount Tabor.

That's not to say there weren't strategic victories. Andrew's forces did capture Caesarea, and the Templars were able to found the formidable Château Pèlerin south of Haifa. This expanded the domains of the Christian Outremer and bolstered its defences. However, by early 1218, Andrew was growing ill and the crusade had lost momentum. While Jerusalem remained out of reach, Andrew's campaign had been modestly successful, and its legacy was to leave the Crusader States in better shape than before he arrived.

While the Hungarians were marching home, the second phase of the crusade was preparing to sail across the eastern Mediterranean to Egypt; and further plans were going ahead to ensure the success of the Fifth Crusade. An embassy was sent to Keykavus, the Sultan of Rum. He was a Seljuk warlord who could have attacked either the Latin

Empire of Constantinople or the northern Crusader States. It was therefore important for the crusade to ensure they didn't end up having a second enemy to fight. Keykavus went one better by allying with the crusade and using this opportunity to expand his own territories at the expense of the Ayyubids. This enabled a total concentration on the complex task in hand.

The initial target was to be Damietta. This was the most important port at the mouth of the Nile Delta. It had been used for centuries as the gateway to the Indian trade routes and was a prize that could be a strategically vital launch point for any further crusading activities. Whoever controlled Damietta controlled the Nile – and could hold the Ayyubids to ransom. Of course, the importance of Damietta was not lost on Al-Adil; the port was a fortress, protected not just with walls and towers but also with canals and river channels, which had resisted numerous attacks over the centuries.

In May 1218 the crusader army landed and was able to quickly set up a defendable camp opposite Damietta. The crusaders had brought siege equipment with them (much as they had in the Third Crusade), and their first target was the so-called Tower of Chains, a defensive tower positioned between the crusader camp and the main walls of Damietta. After multiple assaults and numerous setbacks, the crusaders crept ever forwards and captured this key tower in August. It came as a huge relief to have this firm toehold on Egyptian soil.

The capture of the tower was a major wake-up call for the Ayyubid forces, resulting in a number of counter-attacks on the crusaders' fortified base. Each was pushed back, but the tenuous nature of their predicament was plain for all to see. So in early 1219, a new plan for the complete envelopment of Damietta was carried out. While the crusader forces were stretched thinner, the town was cut off from supplies and fresh troops. Unless relief forces could break through, the countdown for surrender had started.

Al-Adil by now was dead, and the new sultan, Al-Kamil, inherited a land where, in the far north, he faced attacks from the Seljuks. But far more alarmingly, he had a crusade besieging one of his key ports. He poured more troops into the relief of Damietta. The crusade had also had a change of leader, and Pelagius of Albano had arrived as official Papal Legate. The Christians held on tenaciously; they were losing men, but the breakthrough Al-Kamil desperately needed had yet to arrive. What next occurred sounds surreal but actually happened. One of the most celebrated saints of the medieval era, Francis of Assisi, arrived at the crusader camp. Even during his lifetime he was revered as a truly holy person. Francis had correctly predicted that an attack on the Ayyubid camp to the south of Damietta would fail. Because of his evident powers and because he had had a vision in which he converted the sultan to Christianity, Francis was reluctantly allowed to go to Al-Kamil. His mission was an abject failure. His approach had been regarded as an insult to Al-Kamil's faith, and he was unsuccessful in reaching any agreement. All things considered, he had been lucky to escape with his life.

Despite this bizarre moment in history, the inevitable happened in November 1219, when Damietta fell to the crusade after nearly a year and a half of siege. This one had lasted longer than the siege of Antioch during the First Crusade; and while this one had been better prepared, it was equally heroic and as strategically important. Indeed, the fall of Damietta was greeted with huge celebrations across Europe. Once again, the Crusades had been blessed by God.

Except that the crusaders themselves didn't quite see it that way. John of Brienne, the Latin Emperor of Constantinople (technically regent but let's not get distracted), thought Damietta should now be his, but Pelagius saw it differently. Whereas in the past the Crusades had been relatively united by the efforts to gain new territory, Damietta highlighted the split in the army and the contradictory allegiances.

After the squabbling had subsided, the crusade moved on to its new destination, Cairo, the seat of Ayyubid power. Al-Kamil was already on the back foot, and many of his best troops had died in the attempt to relieve Damietta; while the crusade's attempt to take Cairo might have been ambitious, this was the best opportunity they were likely to get for such a campaign.

The Fifth Crusade was one of the most technical ever put together. The First Crusade had blundered into the Middle East and won by blind luck. A lot had been learned in 120 years; there were diplomatic initiatives, plans for naval transportation and, at Damietta, the use of siege engines on both sides. Therefore it's not surprising that Al-Kamil's attempt to stop the crusade was also a technical solution to a military problem.

First, the crusade's northern (Muslim) ally, Keykavus, had been defeated, allowing some Ayyubid forces to head south and relieve the pressure on Egypt. Second, the Nile Delta region is flat and wide open, perfect for horse archers to harass the oncoming crusader army. Because of this, a number of nobles grew tired of the harassment and left. At this point, crusader forces were dwindling and the army was losing momentum. Some advised Pelagius to return to the safety of Damietta to reinforce their considerable advantage in Egypt. He took no notice and ploughed on.

The crux of Al-Kamil's plan was revealed as the crusaders headed further and further away from their base of operations at Damietta. He broke the dams and waterways that tamed the Nile, and the river washed onto the floodplain where the crusaders trudged. Pathways became submerged, tracks became sticky mud. The crusade got bogged down and was rapidly surrounded by Ayyubid troops deep in enemy territory.

Pelagius had no option but to surrender to avoid a massacre. Again, we see a contradiction in the traditional views of crusader/Muslim relations. You would think that the crusaders would have fought to the death, or that Al-Kamil might have wiped out these religious zealots who had been determined to destroy him; but instead, negotiations were conducted for the release of the crusader forces.

The end result was a straight swap. Damietta, which had been such a hard-won gain for the crusade, was returned to Ayyubid rule. In return, the remaining crusaders were free to go, their tails between their legs; years of struggle had produced no tactical gain. The humbled soldiers of Christ began their humiliating journey home in 1221.

The Fifth Crusade, which had started so promisingly, ended in seeming failure; but thanks to events outside of Egypt, the Kingdom of Jerusalem was stronger than before. In fact, the Fifth Crusade was neither a wretched disaster nor a campaign corrosive to the West's influence in the Holy Land. However, the return of Damietta to Ayyubid authority was greeted with huge hostility in Europe, and the outrage focused on the Pope himself. Would it have been more appropriate for the crusade to sacrifice itself so that Damietta remained in Christian hands? This may sound like an odd question, but it's one that plainly crossed the minds of contemporaries.

It's hard to put a date on when interest in the crusading movement began to wane, but the Fifth Crusade undoubtedly made a contribution. It was the last one to be called by the Church and answered by multiple countries of Europe. Later, crusades would have an international element but they were inevitably spearheaded, organised and led by a specific country.

Maybe, after over 100 years of fighting, it was starting to dawn on the general subconscious of Europe that there hadn't been a clear-cut victorious crusade since the first one. The Third had stopped the annihilation of Christian lands in the East but it had failed to reclaim Jerusalem, and the Fourth one hadn't even been fought against Muslims. After the events of the Fifth and Albigensian Crusades, the strong narrative of Christian soldiers smiting the unbelievers, all as part of God's plan, seemed to be a tarnished ideal.

But the Fifth Crusade was by no means the last; and while zeal was starting to give way to political reality, there would be more journeys to the East. Meanwhile, they would have to wait a while for another Muslim crusade – there was some unfinished business closer to home.

8

Blood and Snow: The Northern Crusades

Although Celestine III was pontiff in the 1190s, he's largely forgotten as he wasn't the Pope who called for the Third Crusade and he was succeeded by the hugely important and powerful Innocent III. This is a shame because by the time of Celestine III's rule, the crusading ideal had become ingrained, and it was his preaching of crusade that would result in one of the longest-lasting successes in crusading history.

As already mentioned, north-eastern Europe was still home to the pagans, despite a number of campaigns to push them back. The Teutonic Knights, created late in 1190, was a major military order that would see action in the Holy Land, but one (as the name suggests) that would spend most of its time and effort on the borders of Christian German lands, taking the fight to the pagans.

The concept of converting pagans through military conquest originated with Charlemagne, who spent years in the late eighth century fighting the then pagan Saxons. After much spilling of blood he had been successful, and by the 1190s Saxony was as Christian as Sorrento. It was Celestine III, however, who pulled all these ideas together, and in 1193 called a specific Northern Crusade against the pagans. This was further ratified when, in 1198, he confirmed the foundation of the Order of the Teutonic Knights.

As the Third Crusade had just finished, this new campaign could have been called the Fourth Crusade, but numbers were reserved for targets in the Middle East (although, as we now know, the Fourth Crusade deviated wildly from the original plan). The reason for mentioning this now, rather than earlier, is that, in a similar manner to the Albigensian Crusade, the fighting in this instance dragged on and on. Instead of one crusade, we see generations of Christian fighters pushing into pagan territory, sometimes winning and sometimes losing.

The Christian allies in this endeavour were the kings of Denmark and Sweden (proud of their Viking ancestry, they were also, by now, proud Christians), who supported the Teutonic Knights. To complicate things even further, some Swedish campaigns against Russian Eastern Orthodox Christians were also considered by some to be part of the Northern Crusades. As there had already been a crusade against Orthodox Christians, this idea had more traction after the Fourth Crusade, but it led to complex alliances between pagan princes and Orthodox kings, all fighting against polyglot Catholic Christian armies.

Further, as the time frames can be measured in decades, it's hard to describe any one conflict as either a campaign or even a crusade. So the Northern Crusades have parallels with the Albigensian Crusade; and just as Innocent III never saw the end of that crusade Celestine III was long dead by the time paganism had been wiped out in northern Europe.

Medieval bishops were a little more militant than their modern counterparts. I have already mentioned a number of churchmen who acted as Papal Legates and were obliged to lead or assist on various crusades. These men, although priests, did sometimes fight; they were banned from using any weapon that drew blood – swords, bows and the like – but were allowed to carry maces, essentially clubs with steel heads. Although drawing blood was prohibited, it was fine to crush skulls – in the name of the Lord.

This muscular form of Christianity was personified by Bishop Berthold of Hanover. In 1198 he led the first official crusader force into Livonia (Latvia). They travelled into the area by boat on the now established trading routes from Christian Europe to these pagan lands. The Livonians quickly raised an army to repel the invaders, but, as would be shown time and again, the heavy armour of the crusaders would keep casualty figures low against the much lighter arms and armour of the pagan forces. Berthold's army was victorious, but he had been in the thick of the fighting (presumably using his mace to bring the will of God to the skulls of the heathens) and was badly wounded. When he eventually died of his wounds, this new kind of crusade was left leaderless. As a result, this strategic victory turned into a tactical defeat; for the time being, the crusaders went home.

In 1199, Albert of Buxhoeveden was tasked to Christianise the Baltic pagans. Albert began by garnering support as he travelled around the Holy Roman Empire preaching crusade. He was further aided by a papal bull approved by that most fanatical fan of crusades, Innocent III (this venture would technically mean Innocent started four different crusades). This decree was vital as it declared that fighting against the Baltic pagans was of the same rank as a crusade to the Holy Land.

With only twenty-three ships and 500 soldiers, the first contingent arrived at the mouth of the Daugava in 1200. It was an inauspicious start. However, after the embarrassment of the Fourth Crusade, the German princes were more disposed to assist crusading efforts closer to home. It was simply easier to take a trip which lasted just a few days than to travel for months, at huge expense, to get to the Middle East (if you ever got that far).

This, plus Albert's continued preaching, meant that there

were regular reinforcements. This crusade was seasonal, almost like hunting season; the crusaders usually arrived to fight during the spring and returned to their homes in the autumn. As in the Middle East, the locals had finite resources to combat the crusaders. The crusaders, by comparison, would never be large in number, but could rely on a virtually inexhaustible supply of men and money coming from other lands.

Albert wasn't just interested in fighting. The initial way into the Baltic region had been through trade routes, so markets were set up, markets which were defended and run by the crusade. They proved to be very successful, which meant that as the money flowed into the coffers of the Teutonic Knights, pagan enterprise was strangled. Then Pope Innocent III dedicated the Baltic region to the Virgin Mary to encourage further trade, and even pilgrimage, to the area. It worked – and the area is sometimes still referred to as 'Mary's Land'. The economic war was in many ways even more important than the military one, with many early wins for the crusaders.

However, with the depletion of military forces in the winter months, something was needed to ensure a year-round military presence. In order to further bolster the troops stationed in the Baltic, another, smaller military order was established in 1202. The Livonian Brothers of the Sword was founded specifically and exclusively to fight in northern Europe. Albert was fighting a total war and knew that military action alone would not win the day.

But that's not to say there wasn't fighting. From 1200 to 1212 there were constant sieges and rebellions in Livonia. And as in many earlier battles against the heathens, leaders and men were made to convert. Sometimes it was genuine (after all, the Christ God had clearly bettered the local gods on the battlefield), while others just said what they had to say to fight again another day.

By the mid-1220s Albert was an old man, but Livonia and (most of) Estonia had been conquered and Christianised (in some cases, converted from Greek Orthodox to Roman Catholic). It was now the case that Livonian and Estonian nobles and warriors were joining the military orders and fighting alongside the crusaders against the pagans of other areas. The principle area of interest at this time was northern Estonia, where the extremely belligerent county of Saaremaa was to keep fighting off and on into the 1260s. But as the others in the region were now staunch allies, their loyalties were never questioned after this time. From the point of view of the Pope in Rome, Honorius III, the power and prestige of the papacy had risen significantly, in some ways offsetting the failures of the Fourth and Fifth Crusades.

Albert died in 1229, leaving a hugely potent legacy. There was now a secure base in the Baltic that would operate for generations to come. Livonia and Estonia would be the spearhead into the rest of the heathen lands. It was self-governing and, thanks to trade, self-funding too. As interest in the Middle Eastern crusades waned, many nobles and princes would go on crusade in the north. The story of conflict in this area can be described in decades, centuries if the history of the Teutonic Knights is taken into consideration. They created a semi-autonomous state in northern Europe, which lasted for generations.

But even the Teutonic Knights would find natural limitations to their influence, and to show this we must now look at a new player in the Crusades: the Republic of Novgorod.

Novgorod was then an area that today encompasses parts of Estonia, Belarus and Russia. It was on the hinterland of everything. The population was a mixture of pagans and Orthodox Christians who valued independence above all else.

For decades they had watched as the northern crusaders, the Teutonic Knights and the Livonian Order slowly and inexorably swallowed up their borderlands, one campaigning season after another. So it came as a complete surprise when the Mongols exploded in from the east.

The Mongols have shaped more of Russia's history than outsiders realise. The ethnic group called the Rus' had a capital city of Kiev (founded by the Vikings as a trading post). However, after the Mongol invasion, it was decided that Kiev wasn't convenient, and they made the tiny town of Moscow the central administrative hub for the Rus'. Meanwhile, throughout this period, the Republic of Novgorod was paying regular tributes to the Mongols (the princes of Moscow would also be doing this for centuries to come), a drain on resources when everything was needed to hold back the crusaders. It was a desperate time.

Novgorod's ruler in the early 1240s was the young but hugely energetic leader Alexander Nevsky. The last name means 'of Neva', which he assumed after his first battle and important victory over the crusaders, when he was just nineteen.

In the spring of 1242, the crusaders were marching east into the hinterland of Novgorod. Nevsky rallied all his troops (the battle was not huge, about 4,000–5,000 troops on each side) and they met on the frozen lake of Peipus. So began the Battle of Ice.

Nevsky wanted the crusaders on the ice. While it was a smooth, open surface, their cavalry would find it hard to gain traction (Nevsky had no comparable forces), and the heavy horse regiments of the Teutonic Knights would be neutralised, or at least mitigated.

The battle turned into a slugging match. While the casualty rates for the well-equipped and well-armoured military orders were low, they quickly became exhausted with the effort required to remain upright, in full armour, on ice. After hours of hand-to-hand fighting, Nevsky ordered the archers on either wing of his forces to enter battle. This forced the knights to retreat, in disarray, deeper onto the ice; the appearance of fresh Novgorod cavalry turned a retreat into a rout. When the crusaders eventually regained their composure and attempted to rally on the far side of the lake, they realised that they had inadvertently picked an area of thin ice as the place to concentrate their forces. An ominous groaning noise turned into the sharp sounds of cracking ice, and the smooth surface shattered under the weight of the heavy armour.

While many were able to flee for their lives and others were captured by Nevsky's troops, the freezing cold waters of Lake Peipus were, for a time, a maelstrom of drowning men and horses. The Novgorodians watched limbs thrashing in the freezing water, cries of drowning men and horses echoing around the lake. It was a horrifying and ignoble way for soldiers to die. While the numbers involved were small, the story is one that even the modern reader finds vivid and distressing. To thirteenth-century Christian Europe, it was another huge blow to confidence as pagans and heretics (Orthodox Christians) had won over the righteously led military orders.

The long-term impact from this battle was enormous. The crusader prisoners were eventually released, but only when Novgorod and the Teutonic Knights had established a permanent border through the Narva River and Lake Peipus, thus dividing Orthodox Christians from Western Catholics. The successful defence of Russian territory meant the forces of the Northern Crusade never again mounted a serious challenge to the east and explains why, to this day, Poland is Roman Catholic, while Russia and the Ukraine are Orthodox Christian. Unsurprisingly, Alexander Nevsky was eventually made a saint in the Russian Orthodox Church.

These were the long-term effects, but from Innocent IV's immediate point of view, he was the head of a Church surrounded by enemies; in other words, the enemies of Christ surrounded Europe – and there were even troublesome nobles in Europe.

9

Prester John: The Sixth Crusade and the Storm from the East

The German Emperor Frederick II was known by his contemporaries as 'Stupor Mundi', 'Wonder of the World'. He was of the great Hohenstaufen line that had created such famous figures as Henry II and Frederick Barbarossa, so this Frederick had an illustrious lineage. This was a ruler who could read and speak Latin, German, French, Greek and even Arabic. He was in many ways a Renaissance prince. Unfortunately, he was born about 250 years too early for the actual Renaissance.

It was almost inevitable that this free-thinking, inquisitive, hugely powerful man was going to bump up against the fixed dogma of the Middle Ages; here was a Christian king who could speak the tongue of the infidel! You could almost hear the Inquisition scratching its head. Frederick had come to power after turbulent times, which meant that although he was King of Sicily, Holy Roman Emperor and even (after marrying Isabella of Jerusalem in 1225) titular King of Jerusalem, he knew he could take none of these for granted.

His squabbles with the Vatican, as well as those with his unruly subjects, had kept him from fulfilling his vow to go on the Fifth Crusade; but he had sent troops. Similarly, he actively encouraged subject lords and knights to fight in the Northern Crusades and supported the new military order of the Teutonic Knights, so that by the time he was ready to lead his own crusade, he knew what to expect.

However in 1227, as he set sail, sickness broke out in the ranks, and he chose to return to Italy so his army could recuperate. Enough was enough. The new Pope, Gregory IX, wanted him to stop dithering and get on with it. So as an incentive, he excommunicated Frederick, fearing the whole sickness issue was yet another delaying tactic. Frederick decided to outmanoeuvre the Pope and headed off on crusade anyway. Technically, someone who has been excommunicated can't be a crusader – except that there was a precedent during the Fourth Crusade, when the entire crusade had been temporarily excommunicated and they still marched on.

The Sixth Crusade was the smallest one so far. While Frederick was an emperor, he didn't have the resources of all the princes of Europe combined, in addition to which he was forced to go on crusade quickly, and as a result did not have quite the forces he would have wanted. That said, he was 'Stupor Mundi'. What miracles could he create in the Middle East?

The start of the crusade was not auspicious. Frederick landed in Cyprus, where he managed to alienate the ruling Ibelin family. This meant that one of the most powerful Christian dynasties in the Holy Land would now disengage from the Sixth Crusade, and Frederick's chances of significantly bolstering his forces were diminished. On paper, Frederick obviously didn't have enough troops to inflict the kind of crushing blows that previous crusades had been able to execute.

Frederick also decided a change in tactic from the Fourth and Fifth Crusades. Both of those had Egypt as their intended target. Egypt was the power base of the Ayyubids, so that must be controlled before any attempt to retake Jerusalem could be tried. But Frederick reverted to the plan of earlier crusades. He didn't have the size of force to take on the Ayyubid homelands, so instead he'd make a dash for the ultimate prize. Jerusalem was the ultimate goal, so he would take the shortest route to the Holy Land.

Frederick arrived in Acre, which was now the capital city of the Kingdom of Jerusalem (Jerusalem itself was under Muslim rule). However, Frederick's divisive nature followed him to the new continent. The Teutonic Knights naturally supported Frederick, but the Latin Patriarch of Jerusalem, linked to the papacy, objected to an excommunicate leading a Christian army. The other military orders saw Frederick with his army as exactly the sort of relief force they needed, and yet they, too, were under papal authority so couldn't deal with Frederick. A compromise was struck; the orders of the crusade would not be issued under Frederick's name, which would allow the Hospitallers and Templars a way to join without breaking the taboo of Christians working with excommunicates.

All the wrangling occurred because this was the first crusade where there was no Papal Legate. A number of these legates have been named in previous chapters; they were the spiritual, and at times absolute, leaders of the Crusades. It was the legate who ensured that everyone complied with the Pope's will. That's not to say they were men of peace, but they were at the very least a reminder of the theological nature of a crusade. However, the Sixth Crusade broke this rule and showed that a king could be both leader and legate combined. If the Fifth Crusade was starting to show an unravelling of the crusading ideal, the Sixth Crusade confirmed it.

The advantage was that there were no decisions by committee; there were no tensions because leaders were not jockeying for position. Everything began and ended with Frederick, which is exactly the way he wanted it. He realised that while his army was large, it wasn't big enough for another Damietta, or even another siege of Antioch. However, Frederick, unlike most previous crusaders, was well informed about the state of affairs in the Middle East; and it helped that he could communicate in Arabic, too.

Frederick knew that the current Sultan, Al-Kamil, had tried to negotiate a peace settlement years earlier, and that he was now facing rebellions in Syria. In short, the last thing the sultan needed was a crusade turning up; and even if the force wasn't huge, it could be joined at any time by other Christian lords. Frederick therefore hoped that marching his army south towards Egypt would appear to be a potentially big enough headache to bring Al-Kamil to the negotiating table.

Frederick was bluffing; he didn't have the resources to properly invade Egypt. And while he knew that he could expect no assistance from Europe, he also knew that Al-Kamil wasn't aware of any of this. Frederick understood what it was like to try to stamp out invasions and gambled that he could make a deal with the sultan, one which would let him think that Frederick was out of the picture. From his point of view, Al-Kamil would have one less problem to deal with.

The bluff worked spectacularly. Al-Kamil agreed to hand over not only Jerusalem but Nazareth, Sidon, Jaffa and Bethlehem. The treaty also enshrined a truce of ten years, until 1239. But this was not a deal brokered by a conqueror. Instead, it was a treaty negotiated by two equals, so the victory was not absolute. For example, the Muslims retained control over the Al-Aqsa Mosque and the Dome of the Rock (and therefore the Temple Mount). Perhaps more importantly, Frederick, who was now the actual King of Jerusalem, was not permitted to rebuild Jerusalem's fortifications. However, Frederick could now boast a (controversial) coronation in Jerusalem as the new King of Jerusalem, the first in over a generation to be able to do so.

Like many compromises, it was a treaty designed to please everyone, but ultimately pleased no one. To the modern eye, it's an attractive deal and the best Frederick could reasonably have expected given the circumstances. At a stroke, and without having to fight any pitched battles, Frederick had managed to regain Jerusalem, which had been in Muslim hands since 1187. But to many in Europe, that was missing the point. Infidels should be fought, not bargained with. Surely the reason for a crusade was to battle against Muslims, not sign treaties with them – and following defeat, the crusaders should ensure that Jerusalem was safe from future attack.

Knowing that his unruly empire couldn't be left long without him and satisfied that he had secured Jerusalem, Frederick headed home.

The Sixth Crusade had been one of the shortest, lasting a little over a year. It was also unique in that it was the only crusade where there was no significant loss of life. No battles were fought, no sieges were initiated; and yet, a significant part of the Kingdom of Jerusalem had been restored to the Christians, including some of the holiest Christian sites. On paper, at least, it had been the most successful crusade since the first one. Frederick returned home, invaded Italy and politely asked the Pope to drop the excommunication … which he did.

And yet, the lack of fighting was part of the problem. This crusade had been carried out by an excommunicated emperor, there was no Papal Legate and there were no stories of bravery or battle to retell. While the results were some of the most positive in crusading history, contemporaries almost immediately turned their backs on the events of 1228–29. They didn't seem to fit any kind of understandable narrative. Besides, the truce put an end to any Middle Eastern crusades for a decade. This was a very strange state of affairs. What next? Hell on Earth?

There is a wonderful medieval legend about a ruler called Prester John. Christians in the West were vaguely aware of the fact that some early Christians (most notably St Thomas) went to the East to spread Christianity and that there may have been some erratic communications between Nestorian Christians (an ancient sect of Christianity in Asia) and fellow Christians in Europe. These murky reports appeared to confirm that while the East was clearly full of magical beasts and men with the heads of dogs (this was a genuinely held medieval belief), in the midst of all that was fantastical and alien, the word of Christ was present, too.

And so the legend of Prester John began in the twelfth century and grew ever more embellished as time went on. He was a king and a priest; he was as wise and as wealthy as Solomon; his kingdom was vast. Of course, no legend is complete without fabulous magical objects. He had a mirror that allowed him to gaze on any part of his kingdom (an early version of CCTV); and naturally, a fountain of youth, which would explain his remarkable longevity.

Prester John became wish fulfilment; everything wrong with Europe was fixed in the tale of this legendary ruler. It didn't help that a supposed letter from him circulated throughout Europe, adding hope that he would come to the aid of the Holy Land. Medieval maps were never that accurate at the best of times, but many that show Asia also show Prester John (as well as dragons). In the medieval mind, he was as real and as mysterious as India. In fact, it might well have been the Crusades that sparked these tales in the first place. Why didn't Prester John beat Saladin or save Jerusalem? There was always a convenient flood that stopped him crossing a key river to the Holy Land, but everyone had it on reliable authority that he wanted to help and that he was coming.

The humiliating defeat and incarceration of the Fifth Crusade added fuel to the fire. On his return from captivity,

Jacques de Vitry, Bishop of Acre, came with good news: King David of India, the son or grandson of Prester John, was raising an army. Vitry was basing his information on persistent rumours about the massive defeats of huge and previously unknown Muslim kingdoms in the Far East. They weren't being attacked by any known Christian force, so it had to be Prester John or, in this case, his grandson. Someone was killing Muslims, and surely, the enemy of my enemy is my friend. Right?

Prester John revealed himself to Christian Europe, not in the Middle East but in Europe, in the year 1241. In March, a Polish Christian army was annihilated by an unknown force. The defeat spread panic, and a few days later Krakow was abandoned, sacked and burned. One of the largest cities in the region lay in ruins.

The three main military orders and their allies, including the Holy Roman Empire, were quick to respond; on 9 April, near Liegnitz, they met this terrifying alien army made up almost exclusively of cavalry. Their horse archers were uncannily accurate, and the battlefield was obscured by either a sudden fog or a malevolent contraption that could belch out smoke. The Christian force was not vast, but it had heavy cavalry. In addition, the military orders provided the cream of Europe's well-armed and well-armoured fighting men. This should be enough to stop the unknown force, this menace. But it wasn't. The horse archers feigned retreat again and again, encouraging the allies to break formation and be picked off. The size of the forces involved is unknown; what is known is that, once again, a Christian army was shattered by the Devil's horsemen.

Europe had no time to absorb the defeat at Liegnitz because just two days later the Christian Kingdom of Hungary was invaded, by apparently the same forces (even though it was 500 miles to the south-east). Here, at the Battle of Mohi, King Bela IV barely escaped with his life.

His forces were surrounded and almost totally wiped out. The mysterious attackers proceeded to sack and pillage Hungary for the rest of the year.

Some of the best armies in Europe had been tested and found badly wanting. True, France and England had yet to join the fray; but looking at the capabilities, resources and tactics of those two kingdoms, it was unlikely the outcome would have been any different. It is said that when Pope Gregory IX heard of these terrifying defeats, he fell ill and died in August of the same year (his successor, Pope Celestine IV, lasted only seventeen days before he died, too).

Clearly, the tales of Prester John had been wrong. It wasn't some great Christian civilisation that had been defeating Muslim armies, but devils, demons on horseback. The Book of Revelation in the Bible makes mention of the devil gathering Gog and Magog, groups of unholy men who fight against Christ and the angels in the final battle on Earth. Europe was shattered, waiting for the hammer blow. Nothing could stop this unspeakable evil, and therefore these invaders from the East became known at the time as the sons of Gog and Magog. In essence, they were the armies of the Antichrist, poised to bring about the End of Days (no wonder the Pope died from shock).

This invasion caused widespread fear and alarm throughout the Continent. The resulting shockwave experienced by Europe in 1241 was what the rest of the known (and some of the unknown) world had been enduring for a generation. The Mongols had arrived!

The story of the Mongol Empire is a big one. This was the largest land-based empire the world has ever seen (the second largest in total territory). It was not often that feudal Japan and thirteenth-century Poland faced the same enemy, but they did when the Mongols came to call. It seems that every few hundred years, on the grass steppes of Asia, a group of cavalry archers would unify and ride west. Sometimes they would head into Europe, as they did in the case of the Huns (ironically, the ancestors of the Hungarians) in the fifth century, and the Magyars in the eighth century. A little later, in the eleventh century, the Turks arrived in the Middle East.

Because these nomadic tribes weren't big on writing, it's unclear in most cases what motivated expansion and temporary alliances; but we can guess, as the story of the Mongols has better sources. It starts with a boy called Temujin, who lost his father, the tribal leader, early on in his life. This was a virtual death sentence, as a boy could not lead a clan; his position was a perilous one. However, after learning from numerous defeats and setbacks, he slowly started to win more fights than he lost. At one low point in his early life, his wife was kidnapped; Temujin was faced with either risking everything to try and retake her, or conceding defeat to fight again another day. He chose the latter option. When they were finally reunited, she may have been pregnant by one of her captors. There were always rumours swirling around the legitimacy of Temujin's first son.

Temujin learned a lot from the blunt and brutal life of the warring groups on the Mongolian steppe. First and foremost, it was not necessary to be high-born to be one of his generals; he rewarded loyalty and ability. Later on, this gave the Mongols a huge advantage over feudal armies, where bloodline, rather than ability, was the deciding factor when it came to military leadership.

Temujin also learnt lessons about victory. Those who were unreliable could face execution, but new vassal tribes were given the opportunity to prove themselves. It meant there were incentives to join: promotion, spoils from war, the chance to keep fighting against the rising power in the region. It was an excellent plan. In 1206 Temujin fought the last of his battles against fellow Mongols and had united all the rival clans under one standard (actually, nine horse-hair banners called a tug). In a grand ceremony, he was given the title Genghis Khan, meaning something along the lines of 'powerful ruler'.

So with a honed army, led by experienced and proven generals, Genghis Khan entrenched the unification of the Mongol people by attacking everybody else, declaring that it was the Mongols' divine right to rule the entire world ... and they took it literally!

Therefore, while the Mongols seem peripheral to the story of the Crusades, they affected all the major powers that have been part of the story so far. From 1206 to his death in 1227, Genghis Khan and his generals invaded and took control of northern China, central Asia and the Caucasus. They were spreading out in all directions.

The first Islamic area to encounter the Mongols is the now largely forgotten Khwarazmian Empire. Just because it has been forgotten doesn't mean it was insignificant; it covered an area of land larger than France, Germany and Spain combined. It was a huge central Asian power. Initially their shah paid tribute to the Mongols; but then, in 1218, he carried out a remarkably bold volte-face when he ordered the execution of some Mongol emissaries. This was a deliberate and unforgivable affront to the Mongols.

Between 1218 and 1221 the Mongols carried out what was partly a military invasion of the empire, but also partly a campaign of extermination. This sealed the reputation of the Mongols as inhuman demons whose atrocities were recorded in Muslim chronicles. It was probably echoes of this campaign that Vitry heard about in captivity during the Fifth Crusade.

In the space of three years, the Mongols destroyed this civilisation. Little is remembered about it now because little was left. The Mongols went out of their way to kill and destroy everyone and everything in the Khwarazmian Empire. This was a message to the wider world to say, 'Do *not* mess with us.' One Persian chronicle states that at the massacre at Urgench (a very large and ancient central Asian city), the 50,000 Mongols were told to execute twenty-four citizens each. The maths would indicate a death toll of 1.2 million, a number greater than the actual population, so this was an exaggeration. But there was no getting around the unique levels of destruction the Mongols could wreak when properly motivated. As a result, far more cities threw open their doors to the Mongols (who had a relatively small population, so needed fear as a prime weapon to keep the larger population of conquered peoples submissive) than fought to the end, knowing a massacre would be the outcome.

Genghis Khan died in 1227, after which there was a great gathering to decide his successor. This was important as it meant that, suddenly, all campaigns were put on hold so the armies could be recalled and the generals consulted (and it took a long time to trek all the way back to Mongolia from somewhere like Georgia). Eventually the decision was made to declare Genghis's third son, Ogedai, the next khan.

Skipping ahead to Europe and the winter of 1241, we find that the Mongols had destroyed multiple European armies and had ravaged swathes of eastern Europe. Things were not looking good. Once winter was over, what would stop them from rampaging through the Continent's heartland? Christian Europe held its breath, and then in the spring of 1242 ... nothing. The devil's horsemen were nowhere to be seen.

In Poland this created the legend (still believed by many to this day) that the casualties inflicted on the Mongols at the Battle of Liegnitz were so great that the hordes turned back, fearing ever meeting such fierce resistance again. This may swell a Polish man's heart with pride, but even a cursory reading of Mongol history indicates this was clearly not the case.

All the Mongol battles in Europe were clear-cut and easy wins for the Mongols. If anything, these show how likely and how easy a Mongol invasion of Europe would have been. Instead, the saviour of Europe was, ironically, the very man who wanted it conquered: Ogedai Khan. Ogedai died in the winter of 1241, and it took months for the news to travel west. According to custom, the Mongol armies returned to Mongolia to decide on a new khan.

As the Mongols were a naturally warlike society, the transition from one khan to another rarely ran smoothly. So it was not unusual to fight a long civil war, stretching across the Asian steppes, as one horde fought another over rival claims to rule.

This, in effect, meant a stay of execution for both the Middle Eastern Islamic territories and eastern Europe. Of course, nobody knew why the Mongols weren't rampaging again, but everyone agreed that it was a good thing.

Once the new khan was installed and had crushed all opposition, Mongke Khan initially put all his efforts into conquering Far Eastern territories such as Korea, a very long way from either the Holy Land or Hungary. For the time being, after a huge blow to both Muslims and Christians, the status quo seemed to have returned.

10

To Egypt ... Again: The Seventh Crusade

Once the dust had settled after the shock attack by the Devil's horsemen, Pope Innocent IV did a remarkable thing. In 1245 he sent an envoy, Giovanni da Pian del Carpine, to Mongolia (which, from a medieval European perspective, meant going off the edge of the map and into the complete unknown). Carpine was armed with a papal bull stating that the Mongols should become Christians. Carpine's journey from Europe to eastern Asia was one of the great journeys of discovery. This forgotten man trekked across thousands of miles to face the Devil on Earth and convince him to convert to Christianity. He wrote a story of his journey, which vividly illustrates the enormity of the undertaking he had been given.

Carpine was stunned to find Nestorian Christians at the Mongol court. It turned out that, during this period of Mongol imperial history, all religions were treated equally. While the khans themselves practiced a shamanistic form of belief, Buddhists, Muslims and Christians all mingled in the Mongolian seat of power at Karakorum. But Mongke wasn't interested in Carpine or what the Pope had to say.

Carpine returned to Europe a year later, his mission a failure (although his chronicle is invaluable as a historical record). He brought with him a decree from Mongke Khan stating that Europe should capitulate to him. It was a chilling reminder that the Mongols would not negotiate, and that they were as mysterious as they were unstoppable.

Carpine's mission was probably the only original idea Innocent IV ever had, since a large part of his early reign had been taken up with the by now standard rowing with Frederick II over the power of the Church. Almost as if to underscore his lack of imagination, he resorted to that least original of papal ideas and decreed a Seventh Crusade. With this, he hoped to regain the initiative after Europe had suffered two crushing defeats in as many years (the other being at Lake Peipus with Alexander Nevsky).

Then, in 1244, after the truce of Jerusalem had ended, this most holy city was captured again by Muslims (this time by the Turkic Khwarazmians, displaced from central Asia by the Mongols, who really did change the status quo wherever they rampaged). That the city once again was slipping from Christian hands was not wholly unexpected and didn't cause hysteria in Europe. By now, the whole crusading ideal and the concept of Christ's will being made manifest was looking tattered.

But Christian confidence was struck an even bigger blow just a few months later at the Battle of La Forbie. This clash in October of 1244 shows how diminished the military presence of the Crusader States had become. In this campaign the Kingdom of Jerusalem and the military orders fought side by side with the Ayyubids of Syria against the Egyptian Ayyubids. The crusaders were the junior partners, reduced to auxiliary roles in a larger Muslim army fighting against another Muslim army.

A more positive reading of this battle shows how the Christians of the Holy Land had become far more pragmatic than their European counterparts. Better to side with friendly Muslims to fight the biggest power in the land than fight everyone and guarantee your defeat.

As it was, the Ayyubids of Egypt were led by the

formidable Mameluke general Baibars. The Mamelukes were not a race, but a class of people in Ayyubid society. They were slaves, bought as children (they were either Christian or pagan, as Muslims could not be slaves), converted to Islam and reared to be elite members of the cavalry; they were totally loyal to the ruler of the Ayyubid state. Many had been born in Asia or Russia and had been sold into slavery when the Mongol hordes smashed their way through the region. They were ruthless and fanatical, a force to be reckoned with, particularly when led by the zealous and highly skilled Baibars.

As good as the plan of alliance was for the crusaders, Baibars prevailed and crushed both the local Muslim resistance and the Christian forces. It is the Battle of La Forbie that is seen as the point of no return for the Christians in the Holy Land. Their power had already waned; La Forbie simply confirmed it, and crusader forces never fully recovered. It was an ominous sign of things to come.

So, what better option was there than to declare a Seventh Crusade? And as luck would have it, the new French king, Louis IX, was a man who took his Christian responsibilities seriously and was just aching to go on crusade.

Louis had been on the throne since he was a boy. While his rule had already lasted twenty years, he was still only in his early thirties and at the peak of his powers, both mental and physical.

As with the Sixth Crusade (which established the pattern), the call to arms was less ambitious; rather than trying to rally troops from all over Europe, this was an exclusively French endeavour, supported both logistically and militarily by the Knights Templar.

Thanks to the iron fist of the Albigenisan Crusade, Louis, unlike previous French kings, had the luxury of a relatively united kingdom. This allowed him to raise around 1.5

million livres tournois to fund the crusade, making it one of the most financially sound expeditions so far. With such means he was able to ensure the hiring and equipping of 5,000 crossbowmen. As their bolts were particularly effective against Ayyubid light armour, they would frequently prove their worth in the coming campaign. This crusade would end up being the single largest European invasion in the eastern Mediterranean until Napoleon landed in Egypt in 1798.

Everyone in France seemed to be in the grip of crusading fever, to the extent that a strange footnote crusade, the so-called Shepherds' Crusade, was called. As Louis was sailing off to Cyprus, a Hungarian priest (a bit like Peter the Hermit in the First Crusade) thought he had been visited by angels and implored peasants to join him on a march to Jerusalem. Their journey would surely be blessed by God.

What actually happened was that this poorly organised and impoverished rabble started attacking cities, pillaging small towns and carrying out God's will by assaulting any Jewish communities they could find. It was quickly dispatched by the French authorities, but is a reminder of how powerful the idea of going on crusade was to the whole of European society in the Middle Ages.

For the first time, however, the exact target of the crusade was not to be decided until the crusade itself was on its way. Louis knew the high-risk nature of such a campaign and wanted to make sure that his extremely expensive army would find its way to where it could do the most good – or damage.

Louis arrived in Cyprus, where there were discussions with all the interested parties. The Latin Empire of Constantinople wanted help against the resurgent Byzantines based around Nicaea. It wasn't a bad idea, and they could certainly do with some outside help, but the Fourth Crusade was one of the most tarnished, so there was little appetite to continue that legacy. Besides, Louis was a good medieval Christian and wanted to do battle with a Muslim enemy, not Greek heretics.

As there had been losses in the Kingdom of Jerusalem (most notably Jerusalem itself, but there was also Sidon), there were the expected petitions from the Holy Land. Similarly, the Principality of Antioch was slowly losing its war with neighbouring Muslim powers and was in need of assistance.

All of these were realistic goals for the crusade, except that Louis knew how close the Fifth Crusade had come to cutting the head off the serpent by invading Egypt. Egypt was the key, the power base, the grain basket of the Near East. If he could take Damietta and push inland, it would relieve the pressure on the Christian kingdoms in the East and perhaps prepare the way for more permanent gains in the Holy Land.

The target, then, was Egypt. Much of what happened is vividly described by Jean Joinville, Seneschal of Champagne, who wrote a fairly sycophantic account of Louis's life. Louis instilled great loyalty and confidence in his men, and his landing at Damietta showed incredible coolness under fire. It was the spring of 1249, and Louis knew that an earlier storm had dispersed his fleet, meaning that only about a third of his men were available to land – and yet there was a Saracen army waiting for them. Joinville vividly describes the decision to engage a contested beach with inferior numbers. The knights

> stuck the sharp ends of our shields into the sand and fixed [our] lances firmly in the ground.

This bought the heavily armoured Christian troops enough time and protection to form a beachhead, which the lighter Muslim cavalry couldn't engage, while the crusaders hid behind shields, which kept them safe from missile attack. The expensively purchased crossbowmen earned their pay by taking out some of the Mameluke cavalry.

Once the king's standard was on shore, Louis could wait no longer. He jumped into the sea and, up to his armpits in salt water and weighed down by his battle armour, waded ashore. Everyone else had no option but to follow.

The Muslims knew they had lost their chance to annihilate the crusade before it had even begun. Thanks to Louis's decisive leadership, the Muslim army retreated. Consequently, unlike the Fifth Crusade, this crusade could move quickly and largely unopposed to Damietta. As the Ayyubid army withdrew south, Damietta was left to fend for itself and had no option but to surrender.

An epic siege had been avoided; yet again, a crusade held the power at the very mouth of the Nile. All the retreating Ayyubid troops could do was to burn down the market. On capturing the city, the crusade found fifty-three Christian prisoners who claimed to have been captured during the Fifth Crusade and had been there for thirty years.

Although the crusade did not know this, luck was on their side. As they had done before, they had managed to land at a time when the ruler was not only ill, but slowly dying. With all the turmoil in the Middle East, with power-playing local lords, with a Mongol threat on the horizon and now a crusade in Egypt, weak leadership was the last thing the Ayyubids needed. Things were about to get very messy.

The Muslims knew how to stop a crusade in Egypt once again, the Nile was flooded; the crusade could do little for months. While it is true that had Louis moved quicker, he could have taken advantage of the imminent power vacuum, moving medieval armies was a challenge at the best of times. Now, faced with either slogging through flooded farmland (which had been the undoing of the Fifth Crusade) or trekking through desert wastes, Louis could be forgiven for delaying further action until the path to Cairo improved.

In November 1249, Louis decided to move out with the Templars at the vanguard of the army. He was better equipped than the Fifth Crusade, so while his army was slower, it had food, water and timber to erect defence or bridges if necessary. However, he failed to create supply dumps, which would be vital if he ever needed to make a hasty retreat. Louis was cautious, but not over-cautious. Ironically, just as he began his move south, the sultan died, resulting in a temporary whirlwind of intrigue around the succession.

The crusade arrived at the town of Al Mansurah, where it faced the Mamelukes and the Mamelukes only. Although the crusaders didn't know this, they had just witnessed the passing of authority from an ancient dynasty to a new power in Egypt, one that would last for centuries to come. However, what most mattered at that particular moment was that the Mamelukes were on one side of the river, the crusaders on the other.

Louis ordered the army to dig in, and with further supplies and equipment shipped downriver by his navy, the crusade was able to erect siege engines to fire into the Mameluke camp. The Muslims returned fire, but the palace coup was not complete, and the death of the sultan was still being kept a secret. Because the Muslims were indecisive, the crusaders were able to gain the initiative.

Meanwhile, as there was nobody to negotiate with, Louis had no option but to fight – and besides, Louis didn't plan on handing over Damietta for some kind of truce. So why would he negotiate? He had already achieved more than the Fifth Crusade, and if he broke the army in front of him he knew he would have the upper hand, and maybe even a clear march to Cairo.

By fording the river at a point so deep the horses and riders had to half-wade, half-swim across, Louis's brother,

Robert of Artois, led the Templars in a lightning strike on the Mameluke camp. The plan was a classic outflanking manoeuvre. Robert was going to attack from a direction the Mamelukes wouldn't be expecting.

The crossing was a success, but Baibars, on seeing the Christian cavalry arriving from an unexpected direction, quickly came up with the unique plan of opening the gates of Al Mansurah and letting them in. Once inside, the crusaders had no idea where they were going, or where the main base of the Muslim generals was located. As they scattered along the narrow lanes and streets, they became sitting ducks, perfect targets for ambush.

The crusader force was slaughtered. Of the thousands of men allowed into the town, all but five were killed or captured. Louis could only look on as the cream of his fighting forces fell into a trap and were annihilated. Their screams and shrieks echoed out of the town and across the river where the rest of the impotent crusader army waited. Then, silence. Louis's brother Robert was just one of thousands who died in the fighting.

Louis refused to retreat to the relative safety of Damietta. Having witnessed the near decisive defeat of his forces, he seemed to want to linger in the area and keep some kind of pressure on the enemy. It was an idea that in no way reflected the military reality on the ground.

The new Ayyubid sultan, Turanshah, was far from secure, particularly with the Mamelukes having tasted power, but all agreed the first priority was to get rid of the Christian crusaders. So in order to get around the crusader encampment and cut off its supplies, a small fleet of ships was dragged overland.

Now the crusade was besieged. For months, Louis watched supplies, morale and men fade away. Some Christians even deserted to the Muslim side, the first notable numbers of crusaders to do so. It seems that while Louis had started the crusade as a pious yet realistic leader, the rational part of his leadership had gone. He depended now on prayer and miracles to get them out of this highly dangerous predicament. But God wasn't helping them.

The Muslims used Greek fire on the defences and burned their way into the crusader camp. Louis tried negotiating with Turanshah, at one point desperately suggesting the ridiculous swap of Damietta for Jerusalem, along with safe passage home. It was to no avail. A cornered man has few cards to play, and the Muslims knew it.

Louis fell ill with dysentery and at last conceded that the crusade must return to Damietta. They had been sitting in the same spot for months, under almost constant harassment from a larger army. It was a choice he should have made much earlier.

As the crusaders began to travel north, the Muslims crossed the Nile and caught up with them at Fariskur. Although it is referred to as the Battle of Fariksur, it was really no such thing. Louis's dysentery was so bad he was reduced to cutting a hole in his breeches. The King of France, flower of chivalry, paragon of virtue, had become an incontinent shadow of his former self. Starving, disease-ridden and exhausted, the crusaders put up little fight, and the Mamelukes shattered the remaining Christian force. The whole crusade was encircled and everyone, including Louis, quickly surrendered.

For the first time, the Ayyubids held a Christian king hostage. Louis was well treated, and the sultan brought in a physician to cure his dysentery. Louis was lucky; dysentery could easily kill in a European campaign, but medicine was far more advanced in the Muslim Middle East.

It was in captivity that the crusaders witnessed something unique: the Mameluke coup against their Ayyubid masters. After burning Turanshah's tower sanctuary, they chased him into the river. Joinville describes the scene as an eyewitness:

As the sultan was hurrying to get down to the water, one of these men gave him a lance-thrust to the ribs. He continued his flight with the weapon trailing from his wound ... They ... killed him in the river not far from where our galley lay. [He] cut him open with his sword and took the heart out of his body. Then, with his hands dripping with blood, he came to our king and said: 'What will you give me now that I have killed your enemy. Had he lived, you can be sure he would have killed you.' But the king did not answer him a word.

And with that bloody climax, the Seventh Crusade was over; the Ayyubid Empire was under new management. The Mamelukes had carried out the classic slave revolt and were now lords of all they surveyed.

The Mamelukes were remarkably reasonable in their dealings with the crusaders. Louis was ransomed for 800,000 Bezants (about two-thirds of the annual income of France), but there was no lengthy incarceration, and the bedraggled crusaders were allowed to leave the country in good order. Louis even signed an alliance with the Mamelukes against Damascus (the Muslim force that had earlier fought with the crusaders at La Forbie).

Louis did not return to France. Instead, he set up camp in Acre and spent the next four years bolstering defences for the Christians in the Holy Land. He financed numerous improvements and even installed a permanent garrison in Acre that would be paid for by the French Cown, in theory, forever.

But no king can afford to be out of his country indefinitely, and by 1254 it was time to go home.

However, Louis's involvement with the Crusades was not over yet. Louis was later canonised, the only French king to become a saint.

On the surface, the Seventh Crusade appears to be another disaster, but was it? The Second Crusade was much worse, as it not only failed in its objectives but also left the Crusader States more vulnerable. While Louis's military campaign was an undeniable failure, thanks to his years of excellent leadership and expenditure in Acre, he left the Christian East in a stronger state than he had found it. The crusaders also had a new ally in the Mamelukes, and while there was always going to be a question of trust around a Muslim ally, for the time being Christians in the Holy Land did not face a unified foe. Instead, with multiple competitors all vying for an advantage, no one was targeting the Christians.

And things were about to get a whole lot worse for the Muslims ...

11

They're Back! More Mongolian Mayhem and the Rise of the Mamelukes, 1256–70

The shock waves from the Mongol expansion into central Asia and beyond had been felt throughout the known world; but for more than a decade, things had been quiet in the Muslim Middle East.

From the point of view of many regions in the world, it was the sporadic nature of the Mongol attacks that made them especially terrifying. Just when it seemed they were never to be seen again, tens of thousands of horsemen would arrive apparently from nowhere and mercilessly advance on their target.

The truth was that the Mongols, under their new leader Mongke Khan, had been very busy, but in the Far East. Korea had been smashed, the Mongols had pushed further into the heartland of China, Tibet capitulated and even Vietnam had become a vassal state.

With almost all of southern Asia now under Mongol control, it was time to turn back to the Middle East – and they did so with spectacularly bloody madness in the 1250s.

The first Muslim error occurred when the Assassins sent a death squad to kill Mongke and failed. Even if they had succeeded, it would have made no difference; the Mongols would always avenge such an insult to their prestige.

As previously stated, the Assassins may have been small in number but they had a virtually impregnable string of castles and forts in modern-day Iran and Syria. Their remote locations in arid areas meant that only the most tenacious and well-prepared armies would have any chance of carrying out a successful siege, and they weren't a big enough threat to be worth that level of effort. But that's not the way the Mongols looked at things.

Hulagu was one of Genghis Khan's grandsons, and while he was not the great khan he undoubtedly had the family skills to become a supreme general, not to mention that he was backed by all the resources of an empire in its prime. In 1256 he was campaigning in Iran and planning to head next into the Middle East. However, he did make a special stop at Alamut. The Assassins didn't have a capital city (they were never numerous enough for that) but if they had a centre of power, Alamut was it. It was destroyed after a vigorous siege, and Hulagu marched its occupants, along with those of other Assassin strongholds (conquered in various sieges and raids), into the desert. They all died; whether by sword, arrow or thirst, the outcome was the same.

A few Assassins survived, and there are references to them into the 1270s, but it was Hulagu who destroyed their power base. Their descendants are the Ismailis, a sect of Shi'a Islam led by the Agha Khan. Today they are a peaceful sect of Islam; their days of murder are long behind them.

It could be said that the destruction of Alamut did everyone a favour. The Assassins had attacked the Christians, the Muslims and even the Mongols, but what happened next devastated the Islamic Middle East.

There has never has been an Islamic equivalent of the Pope. Different sects have leaders, but even they tend to be more spiritual leaders than rulers. The closest position in Islam to a unifying religious leader in the thirteenth century was the caliph. The Abbasid caliphs, based in Baghdad, could trace their lineage to the early days of Islamic empire-building in the eighth century AD. While their power waned as that of other ethnic groups emerged (particularly the Turks, as opposed to the Arab rulers in the Middle East), the caliph was the unifying force in Islam in the 1250s.

Baghdad was an ancient city with huge walls and an ancient legacy for being nearly impregnable. The current caliph was Al-Musta'sim, and as Hulagu approached Baghdad he received an ultimatum from the Mongols. Al-Musta'sim rejected the ultimatum, sat behind his thick walls and waited for the inevitable. He made no plans or preparations, an extremely foolhardy failure as he had deliberately snubbed the Mongols; if they were victorious, he could expect no mercy.

Hulagu arrived in January 1258. The city was rapidly enveloped by over 100,000 troops (not just Mongol but from other regions of the empire, too) and Hulagu demonstrated that the Mongols were not only master horsemen but had now embraced the art of siege warfare, too. The Mongol army built a ditch and palisade (wooden wall) around the city. This stopped any chance of escape and also limited the options of a relief force. Then they set up siege engines to pound the walls. The people of Baghdad could not escape, but had to sit and take it. After a few weeks of barrage, it became clear that Baghdad was going to fall. Al-Musta'sim called for talks on surrender; Hulagu declined them. The rule was simple: immediate capitulation and unconditional surrender would save life, but resistance was met with annihilation. The caliph had chosen the latter and had failed to make any preparations for it, making him one of the worst military leaders in history.

The fall of Baghdad in 1258 isn't widely remembered in the West, but it was a tremendously important event with massive implications. Al-Musta'sim was found and brought to Hulagu for judgement. The Mongols had a sacred rule that the blood of a king or emperor should never be shed on the ground, so the Mongols rolled the caliph into a rug and rode their cavalry over him. The honour of this execution was probably lost on Al-Musta'sim. He was kicked to death by hundreds of hooves, his muffled screams the last sounds a caliph would ever make.

The death of Al-Musta'sim marked the end of the Abbasid Caliphate, which had lasted 500 years and was never replaced (the Ottoman sultans would take the title from the sixteenth century onwards, but while they had supreme authority in their realm their caliph 'credentials' weren't recognised by other Muslim rulers). Throughout the era of the Crusades, Islamic scholars had been well ahead of their Western counterparts; while the caliph's death didn't cause the decline of Baghdad, it is seen as the end of the golden age of Islamic learning.

For centuries, Baghdad had stored thousands of books and manuscripts and was one of the key centres of Islamic learning. In fact, it was one of the greatest centres of learning in the world, and the Mongols deliberately destroyed everything. One eyewitness recounted seeing the Tigris run black with the ink from books as so many had been thrown into the river. As a result, countless primary sources were forever lost to future historians.

Although the intellectual loss was great, the human loss of life was even worse. Arab sources estimated the death toll at 200,000. It's tempting to see this as an exaggeration, perhaps meant to underline the enormity of the devastation … until you read that the Mongols claimed 800,000 deaths. The streets were greasy with human fat for weeks afterwards, the horses slipping on it wherever they went in the city. The death and destruction were so great that even the Mongols couldn't stand it, and for the only time in Mongol history they moved out of a city they had only just ravaged, away from the site of their orgy of murder and the overwhelming stench of decay. This was one of the worst massacres in human history.

Unbelievably, it got worse. The Mongols were so determined to leave a permanent scar on Mesopotamia and Persia that they deliberately destroyed the ancient canal systems feeding hundreds of thousands of acres of soil from great rivers like the Euphrates and the Tigris. Today we think of central Iran and Iraq as barren, but they weren't always like that. It was the Mongols' destruction of the irrigation systems, along with the legacy of hugely reduced populations, that allowed farm land to shrivel up, blow away and become desert. It was one the greatest pre-industrial ecological disasters in history, one that still has not been fixed over 700 years later.

The Islamic world had had its cultural and spiritual heart torn out by the Mongols. Could nothing stop these monsters? Some historians have said that Islam was teetering on the brink. I dispute this. The Mongols had no interest in forcing their shamanistic religion on anyone, or in stopping any of the religious practices of their subjects. The beliefs of Islam weren't threatened, but it is fair to say that the Muslim dynasties of the Near East were facing an existential threat like no other.

The Christians in the Holy Land could only look on in horrified fascination. By now the crusaders could muster an army of maybe 5,000–10,000. The Mongols had an army of over 100,000. The Christians stood no chance. Was this yet another case of 'My enemy's enemy is my friend'?

Bohemund VI of Antioch was one ruler who thought so. His family had been in loose diplomatic talks with the Mongols for a while, and Bohemund saw this Mongol invasion as a chance to back the winning team. He made Antioch a vassal state to the Mongol empire, and when Hulagu attacked Syria in 1260, Bohemund and his men provided a minor ancillary force to the Mongol army.

Christian crusaders and the Devil's horsemen riding side by side against a Muslim foe ... the Crusades had unquestionably changed from Urban II's original idea.

The great cities of Aleppo and Damascus were the Mongols' next targets, and they fell easily. The news of Baghdad preceded Hulagu, and as the Mongols had calculated, one massacre can lead to many cities flinging open their gates and suing for peace. The capitulation of these cities effectively ended the Ayyubid Caliphate in the north (the caliphate in the south had already been destroyed by the Mamelukes).

This rapid surrender was the chief reason for the Mongols' success. Although they had several large and highly trained armies, they had a small population compared to many areas of the world; therefore, if every Mongol target had fought to the bitter end, the attrition would have led to Mongol gains fading away as their troop levels declined. But was it worth sacrificing your city and your life (and that of your family) to help the next city along the road? It was a clever piece of psychology.

Now there were crusader soldiers marching into cities which had, for a century and half, eluded them. Bohemund was a minor player in events and was never going to be rewarded with large prizes, but Antioch was given a number of key forts and towns in northern Syria as a sign of gratitude. Bohemund's plan was working, and the key cities that had always threatened Christian lands in the north of Syria were now held by allies ... terrifying and bellicose allies, but allies none the less.

Hulagu knew that the only viable remaining opposition was the new Mameluke regime in Egypt. He sent ambassadors to Cairo to demand capitulation or face the consequences. Sultan Qutuz had the envoys killed. As far as the Mamelukes were concerned, surrender was not an option.

By now Hulagu had conquered huge swathes of Persia, Mesopotamia and Syria. His forces needed consolidation. So he kept the bulk of his force in the north, while he sent his general Kitbuqa (a Nestorian Christian) with two tumens (that's 20,000) of Mongol cavalry south to probe the Mameluke forces.

In the meantime, Sultan Qutuz and General Baibars, the two main leaders of the coup against their old masters, were determined to stay in power and rallied the largest army they could muster. The Mamelukes knew that they faced an enemy which had never been beaten in open battle, one that would show no mercy. Here it's important to remember that the Mamelukes had been raised as warriors, and their horse archers were comparable in skill and tactics to the Mongols. It is also likely that Qutuz and Baibars had been sold into slavery as the result of earlier Mongol raids, so there may have been certain personal dimensions to this conflict as well. The stage was set for a titanic clash.

While all this was going on, the once promising cooperation between the Mongols and the Christians soured. The Count of Sidon foolishly attacked the town of Damas, which was garrisoned by a small number of Mongols. It was a minor skirmish but one of Kitbuqa's grandsons was killed. The Mongols could not let something like this go unpunished, and the city of Sidon was sacked.

This was an indication (if one were needed) that the Mongols were never going to be reliable allies. Their goal was global conquest; it's impossible to ally with a group who has a goal like that. Pope Alexander IV certainly saw it as an unholy alliance, and forbade any further deals with the Mongols. So, when the Mamelukes sent envoys to Acre to ask for the safe passage of their forces through crusader territory (on their way to meet the Mongols), the crusaders (after some dissent and discussion) agreed.

The Mongols, despite being erstwhile allies, were seen as

the greater danger. The events at Liegnitz and in Hungary were still fresh in the minds of the Europeans. They would also have been aware of what had happened in Baghdad; while that was an atrocity against Muslims, the Mongols clearly had no qualms about who they annihilated. The Muslim dynasties of the Middle East, by contrast, had rules and could be reasoned with. Saladin hadn't massacred the Christian population of Jerusalem; Frederick II had been able to negotiate Jerusalem's return; and more recently, Louis IX had been well treated in captivity. Would the Mongols have done any of that? It was doubtful. The Christians decided it was a case of 'better the devil you know'.

So the Mamelukes were granted free access through Christian lands to go to war with the Mongols. Meanwhile, Sultan Qutuz had managed to rally an army of roughly 20,000, approximately equal in size to that of the Mongols. It must have been an ominous sight to the crusaders as they watched their Muslim neighbours ride past their strongholds with an army they could never hope to match.

Then, on 3 September 1260, the Mongols met the Mamelukes at Ayn Jalut. The name is roughly translated as 'the well of Goliath', as the mighty giant from Biblical times was supposed to have rested by a spring in the area. It was an aptly heroic name because the Battle of Ayn Jalut was one of the most important battles in history. It would also have important implications for the Crusader States, even though no crusading army was present on the battlefield.

Baibars was in the lowland region with a small part of the Mameluke force. Both the Mongols and the Mamelukes tried the classic strategy of charging within arrow range, firing volleys from their recurve bows and then feigning retreat to try and lure the enemy. It must have been like looking at mirror images. Similar-sized armies, similar tactics and both sides highly mobile. Eventually Baibars succeeded in luring the Mongols into the highlands, where Qutuz was waiting with the bulk of the Mameluke forces.

The Mamelukes tried enveloping the Mongol army, but the Mongols fought so fiercely that the left wing of the Mamelukes began to crumble under the sheer energy of the Mongol attacks. When Qutuz saw this, he joined this wing with the reserves, flinging off his own helmet so his troops could see their sultan leading the charge.

The Mamelukes did just enough to push back the Mongols; and in the vicious melee, Kitbuqa was killed. The loss of their general dealt the Mongols a psychological blow. By the end of a bloody day, the Mongol force was all but destroyed or fleeing. The Mamelukes had earned their hard-won victory. Casualty numbers are unknown, but they were obviously heavy; and for the very first time, the Mongols had lost a battle. Even though, from a Mongol point of view, this had involved little more than a scouting army and the victory had been narrow, it was a blow to their reputation as invincible. For the Mamelukes, this sealed their reputation as the premier military power in the Middle East. It also gave them the incentive and the momentum to keep pushing north and reclaim some of the Muslim land that had been held by Hulagu. The crusaders may have got rid of the Devil's horsemen, but they were now in danger of being encircled by a unified Muslim empire run by some of the most formidable warriors in the world.

The universal approval Sultan Qutuz enjoyed after his victory over the Mongols was short-lived. On his return to Cairo, he was killed by his own generals. Although Baibars was not at the scene, he was plainly the man behind the plot. Quite why this extremely effective partnership came to such a bloody end will always remain a point of speculation; but it is obvious that Qutuz had inadvertently insulted Baibars in some unforgiveable way.

So the leadership of the Mamelukes, which had been taken in bloodshed, moved to another Mameluke under similar circumstances.

But let's pause for a moment and consider what would have happened had the Mongols won the battle of Ayn Jalut. The destruction of the Mamelukes would have seen the demise of a dynasty that, in reality, lasted into the sixteenth century. It would have meant that the whole of the Middle East was now Mongol territory, and we know there would have been at least another generation of Mongol expansion. Under the circumstances, it's hard to see the Crusader States lasting anything more than another couple of years. Further, the Ottomans were able to rise to power because of the power vacuums occurring in the Middle East (more on that later). With Mongol hegemony this wouldn't have happened, and Osman and his followers would have just been another bunch of mercenaries for hire. So, no Mameluke Sultanate, no Ottoman Empire – and it is not wild speculation to say that had the Mongols wanted to head west, there would have been nothing to stop them.

Further, and without getting too carried away, had the Mongols won at Ayn Jalut, they would probably have wanted the biggest and richest city in Europe – Constantinople. They had conquered larger cities in Asia, and there would have been nothing to stop them heading in this direction, either. So rather than falling to the Ottomans in 1453, Constantinople would probably have been captured by the Mongols by 1280, quite possibly accompanied by a Baghdad scale of destruction.

By looking at events in this way, it is impossible to overestimate the significance of the Battle of Ayn Jalut.

Baibars had led the way in defeating not only the Seventh Crusade but the Mongols, too. This impressive military leader was now Sultan Baibars, and he was to pour his efforts into attacking the Christian kingdoms in the Near East. By the mid-1260s, these kingdoms were hanging on by their fingernails. Was it time for another crusade?

12

The End Game, 1270–91

The Eighth Crusade was, uniquely, not triggered by a papal decree, but by Louis IX's declaration that he intended to take the cross again and make up for his efforts on the Seventh Crusade. Naturally the Church agreed, and Louis again showed the sensible side of his nature as he spent years making preparations. He built up his resources through taxation so that he could raise another fleet, and then he allied with the heir to the English throne, Prince Edward (who would later be Edward I 'Longshanks'). Louis even co-funded Edward's involvement, clearly hoping for more men not only from his English lands but from his lands in France as well (at this time the English royal family had huge estates in France).

This crusade was very much Louis's show. From the time of the Sixth Crusade, the organisation and planning of crusades had devolved from the papacy to the king who was taking the cross. Indeed, Pope Clement IV, knowing that Henry III was getting old and England was only just recovering from a civil war, was not best pleased that the heir to throne was going on such a dangerous campaign.

Louis's crusade was being preached when terrible news reached Europe: Antioch had fallen. Militarily, commercially and spiritually important, the city had been in Christian hands since the time of the First Crusade. Now it had fallen to Baibars.

The story was a sinister one. While the defences were in good order, the garrison was not big enough to properly defend the miles of wall. Consequently, the inhabitants sued for peace with Baibars, agreeing to surrender the city in return for safe passage. This was a standard arrangement to which even the Mongols would often agree. Baibars, not wanting a protracted siege, also agreed. However, when his troops marched in, he barred the gates and sent the Mamelukes on a bloody rampage. All the Christian inhabitants were either massacred or sold into slavery. Almost an entire city's population vanished.

This was the most disgraceful act of brutality ever shown by any Muslim ruler during the Crusades. Looking at the previous centuries of conflict between Muslims and Christians, almost invariably the Christians had behaved in more bellicose and bloodthirsty ways. Now, after decades of brutalisation, Baibars was returning the favour.

In the West it is Saladin who is the poster boy for medieval Muslim military prowess, but Baibars is the one who gets the accolades in the modern Middle East. It's not hard to link some of the fiery rhetoric used by certain people today with the bloody efficiency of Baibars. It's with him that we start to see the uncompromising clash of civilisations surprisingly absent from most of the other crusades.

Europe needed to act and all eyes were on Louis, a man in his fifties, an age considered to be fitting for a king. He was the man to settle the score for Christianity.

However, Louis was being even more cautious than those in previous crusades. There was no point sailing straight to Acre, and Damietta had been attacked twice with disastrous results on both occasions. This time the target would be a Muslim state, which, once secured, would allow an easier line of attack on Egypt. The destination was Tunis.

Tunis was chosen not only as a kind of halfway house

between Europe and Egypt, but also because there was a general feeling (particularly among the Dominican friars) that Tunis wasn't overly enamoured with Islam and was ripe for conversion to Christianity. This may sound insane today, but don't forget that St Francis of Assisi had gone on the Fifth Crusade to Egypt, with the genuine intention of converting the sultan.

The crusade set sail in the late spring of 1270 and landed in Tunis in July, one of the hottest months of the year in North Africa. The crusaders, who were largely accustomed to fighting the European way, dripped with sweat and passed out with heatstroke as they slow-cooked inside their metal armour.

While the idea of conversion was optimistic, the crusade had been well planned. However, it was odd to overlook what the most learned people knew: that North Africa was an oven in the summer. No one knows why a cooler, more inclement time wasn't chosen.

Illness is always a danger to any military encampment, and this is invariably amplified by heat. Therefore, quite predictably, the crusaders very quickly became less concerned with the Emir of Tunis's army (which was nowhere to be seen) and more concerned about the spreading illness in the camp.

August brought more sickness and Louis IX, too, fell ill. The outlook for the French king was bleak; and on 25 August 1270, Louis died from 'flux of the stomach'. His dying words were said to be 'Jerusalem' (although the priest who gave him his last rites and last confession makes no mention of this). Such imagery might be regarded as a little romantic and illustrated a singularity of purpose, but in practical terms it shattered the plans of the crusade. Its leader and main financial supporter was dead. It was time for the bulk of the forces to head home.

There were two spin-offs from these events. First of all, there was a treaty with Tunis that allowed religious freedom for Christians; and in this sense, the crusade had a positive legacy in North Africa. The Tunisian Muslim forces did skirmish with the crusader camp, but they never reached the critical mass of a battle. Surely, in the meantime, wasn't it better to agree to a face-saving treaty with the Christians than to risk a pitched battle? So cooler heads prevailed, and Louis's campaign in Tunisia ended with civilised agreements, rather than conquests.

The second outcome was that Prince Edward decided he still hadn't really been on crusade; and so the heir to the English throne, along with Charles, Count of Anjou (Louis IX's brother), sailed east to Acre. This had never been part of the original plan and is sometimes referred to as the Ninth Crusade. After all, this was a different leader landing on a different continent, so it's not unreasonable to give it another title. But some historians see this as the second part of the Eighth Crusade because it was carried out by some of the forces specifically mustered for that crusade. Either way, there was still a Christian army in play in the Middle East.

In reality, this was the rump of an already small crusading force. Their fleet constituted just thirteen ships; therefore, we can estimate a fighting force of roughly 1,000 men. Edward and Charles's forces were never large enough to seriously tip the balance in the Christians' favour. Instead, Edward ignored the previous papal decrees and reached out to the Mongols in an attempt to find a counterbalance to Baibars. It was a smart piece of diplomacy and the start of Edward's reputation as a wise diplomat (a part of his contemporary reputation that has been forgotten).

As it was, the Mongols were busy with their own internal feuds. Such a pugnacious society meant frequent civil wars; and while there was an agreement in principle, when it came to it, just one tumen (10,000 men) was sent into Syria. The Mongols ravaged the lands around Aleppo, but not much else.

Edward had been hoping to raise Baibars' siege of the strategic Christian town of Tripoli. Bohemund VI may have lost Antioch, but he was hanging on at Tripoli. The Mongol threat did not detract Baibars from his goal of crushing yet another pocket of Christian resistance, and while the main siege dragged on, Mameluke armies had been capturing all kinds of Christian towns and fortifications around Syria. This included the siege of the key Hospitaller castle of Crac des Chevaliers in 1271. It was slowly ground down by siege weapons, and the garrison was hopelessly outnumbered. However, Crac was so well designed that even after a two-month siege it took trickery to end it. The garrison received false orders from their Grand Master to surrender, so they did. Most unusually, Baibars showed restraint and spared their lives.

It was, however, Edward and Charles's arrival that gave Baibars pause for thought. Edward may have known that his forces were small and that there would be no reinforcements, but Baibars didn't. All he knew was that another crusade had arrived, and while it had been a long time since a crusade had conquered and held large tracts of land, he was also aware of the destruction one could cause.

Baibars decided that caution was the best tactic. The Christians got the truce they so badly needed, and Tripoli was saved.

Edward remained in the Holy Land, and it was during this period of prolonged stay that one of the remaining Assassins targeted him. I detailed this in my first book, *The Busy Person's Guide to British History*, but it's such a good story that it's worth retelling.

A merchant came to Edward's court and convinced him that his mission was so delicate he should meet Edward on his own in his private quarters. This guaranteed that Edward would have no armour, shield or sword. His bodyguard detail, while close, wouldn't be close enough to help with a surprise attack.

Once alone, the Assassin lunged at Edward and a brutal close-quarters fight ensued. Edward eventually beat the Assassin to death with a wooden stool, but he fell ill from the wounds he received from the Assassins' infamous weapon of choice, a poisoned dagger. Although likely to be apocryphal, it is said that his wife Eleanor tried to suck the poison from his wounds and carefully attended to the needs of her injured husband.

It was a close-run thing, and it wouldn't have taken much more for Edward to die; had he perished, he would have been a footnote to medieval history rather than one of its giants. However, Edward survived, and he spent his further time in the Holy Land either funding certain improvements or going on raids against small Mameluke outposts and towns. Edward's time there echoed that of his great uncle, Richard the Lionheart, except the scales were different. Both knew that they did not have the men and resources to make any further conquests, so they patched up the Christian kingdoms as best they could. But unlike Richard, Edward had a lot less at his disposal.

Edward's crusade (the Eighth, Part 2 – or the Ninth, whichever you prefer) did the best it could for an unplanned expedition, but it was too little, too late. By the time he sailed home in 1272 there was a ten-year truce in place, but the Crusader States were now all but surrounded by the Mamelukes, the imperial force that had beaten the once invincible Mongols. The future looked undeniably bleak.

In 1284 Pope Martin IV declared a new crusade. Was it against the Muslims? No. Was it against the pagans in Europe? Wrong again. Against Greek Orthodox Christians? Not even close. Heretics? Sorry, they were all dead.

This time it was against the Kingdom of Aragon, one of the kingdoms that, for generations, had been fighting against the Muslims in Iberia. It was triggered when Peter III of Aragon invaded Sicily, technically a papal property. Pope

Martin IV's view was that an attack on Sicily was an attack on the papacy, making Peter every bit as much a threat to good Christians as Baibars. Of course, Peter was no such thing. If it is possible to argue that the Albigensian Crusade muddied the waters between a 'crusade' and a bog-standard political war, then the so-called Aragonese Crusade is where the rot really set in. In reality, Pope Martin IV was simply trying to rally the good Christians of Europe to fight his wars against an enemy he chose. This is something very different from the concept Pope Urban II had envisioned nearly 200 years earlier.

Unsurprisingly, Christian Europe did not leap at this offer. In the end France and a number of other counties and duchies joined forces against Peter, but they were all neighbours, keen to stop Peter from getting too powerful. None of this had anything to do with *Deus Vult*. At first things went well for the 'crusaders', but as supply lines stretched and disease set in, Peter took advantage of fighting on his home turf and won back all he had lost. It was all over in the space of a year or so.

This minor medieval war was important for two reasons. First of all, it showed how politicised the idea of crusade had become. Whatever you may think of the men on the First Crusade, they must have possessed genuine religious zeal to march from Europe to Jerusalem, enduring some of the harshest and most punitive conditions it is possible to encounter when campaigning.

Now crusades were being called for almost routinely, for more and more spurious reasons. It's not difficult to understand why Europe failed to get excited about Aragon invading Sicily.

The second point has to do with the situation in the Holy Land, for what remained of the Crusader States was in critical condition. A crusade on the scale of the First or Third (including Barbarossa's forces) was needed and needed now.

But Europe was far more concerned with local affairs than with rallying a mighty force in the name of God to smite Saracens.

Martin IV was distracted with local issues when he should have been far more worried about the truce with the Mamelukes running out. If he had the chance to call just one crusade, the need was greatest in the East, not in Aragon. If the Pope didn't seem to worry about the Christians in the Holy Land, why should anyone else?

In the 1280s, the Christians in the East were far from unified. The Greeks had overthrown the Latin rulers of Byzantium, and there were new Orthodox emperors, hostile to the Christians in the Holy Land. That said, both the Crusader States and the Byzantines had a common concern: the growing power of the trading states in Italy and their increasing influence in these Christian links to the Asian trade routes.

Pisa, Genoa and Venice were bitter rivals, trying to control Mediterranean and Black Sea trade. They would happily ally with anyone who gave them an edge over one of their competitors. As the Genoese had helped the Byzantines overthrow the Latins in Constantinople and install a new series of Greek emperors, they had the advantage there; for their part, the Venetians were doing their best to gain an advantage in what remained of the Kingdom of Jerusalem.

The scheming was constant and rifts were nurtured, not healed. In the meantime, the Mamelukes were only getting stronger and the Middle East was, once again, unified under a strong military force. For the Christians in the Holy Land, the outlook was dire.

At the same time as the Aragonese Crusade was winding down, the Mamelukes were on the move again. Baibars had died a few years earlier, so in 1285 the Christians were attacked by the new Mameluke leader, Qalawun. Their target was the imposing Hospitaller castle of Margat. Built on an extinct volcano, this castle was second only to Crac des Chevaliers in terms of design and invulnerability.

But no fort is invincible. If there is no attempt to relieve the garrison and the besieging army is large enough, with enough provisions, all defences will eventually fail. The question is how much effort is needed to overcome the defences. The Hospitallers had a garrison numbered in the hundreds, versus an army of over 10,000.

With the Kingdom of Jerusalem a shadow of its former self, no serious relief force would be forthcoming. The Hospitallers knew they would have to fight alone.

Using a method called 'sapping', Qalawun ordered multiple tunnels to be dug under the imposing walls of Margat. Once completed, these tunnels would be kept up with wooden frames, then the wooden structures would be set alight and the lack of support for the wall would lead to collapse. It was dangerous, claustrophobic and dirty work – and in this case the sappers (the men doing the tunnelling) were hacking away at the soft volcanic rock the castle was built on, and not firmer earth.

Thirty-eight days into the siege, one of the tunnels was deliberately collapsed, bringing down part of the south wall. The Hospitallers realised this would be the first of many such attempts to overcome their defences, so they negotiated a generous settlement with Qalawun and were allowed to leave the castle with everything they could carry. No massacre or imprisonment for them.

The greatest compliment Qalawun paid to the Hospitallers was that he did not destroy this formidable castle, but instead repaired and garrisoned it. It was seen as such an important defence that it would be used for centuries to come.

But this was just the beginning for Qalawun. In 1287 he took the Christian-held town of Latakia, and in 1289 he was at the gates of Tripoli. He brought with him a large and well-provisioned army and siege catapults.

In a rare show of solidarity, the Genoese and Venetian galleys in Tripoli at the time cooperated in the defence of the city. Acre sent their French garrison (still being paid for by the French Crown, even though Louis IX had died years before). The Hospitallers and the Templars mustered what troops they could, hoping to stop the Mamelukes. King Henry II of Cyprus, who had also been an actual King of Jerusalem, sent troops, while also accepting civilians fleeing from Tripoli. Qalawun's campaign produced, even to contemporaries, the sense of an endgame.

Meanwhile, the new Pope, Nicholas IV, did nothing. He was spending most of his time on the political wrangling over the ownership of Sicily. Apparently, God's will had moved from the Middle East to a large island off the Italian mainland.

As the West dithered, Qalawun ordered his siege engines to topple towers and tear down walls. The incessant bombardment cracked and crumbled Tripoli's defences. After a little more than a month, Qalawun was ready to send in his assault troops.

The well-prepared Mameluke troops attacked the city walls and quickly pushed their way in against the beleaguered defenders. Battle quickly turned to butchery. Thousands of civilians were massacred; the rest, including women and children, were sold into slavery.

Tripoli had the longest history as a Christian crusader city. It had been run, uninterrupted, for 180 years by the Counts of Tripoli, and its loss horrified the West. But Qalawun wasn't done; Christian Tripoli was a stain that had to be removed. He ordered the entire city to be razed to the ground, and he further ordered a new Tripoli to be built further inland, miles away from the original.

Henry II of Cyprus sent a delegation to Pope Nicholas IV to ask for urgent assistance in the Holy Land. While Nicholas IV agreed, he did not call for a crusade. He was distracted by European politics and perhaps assumed that after nearly 200 years of Christian forces in Outremer, they would somehow hang on. Instead of forces, he sent letters to the monarchs of Europe requesting help. But a begging letter does not have the same urgency as a call for crusade, and nobody did anything. Henry was on his own.

The only major city left was Acre. The trigger for the Mameluke attack on that city turned out not to be Muslim provocation, but Christian folly. During a drunken brawl at the docks, both Christians and Muslims were killed. Qalawun, as the protector of Muslims in the area, demanded the perpetrators be brought to him so he could determine the facts and deliver justice. The Christians argued. Some thought they should comply with these not unreasonable demands, while others thought this was a chance to resist a tyrant.

The debate lasted too long. Impatient to receive an answer, Qalawun mobilised against Acre. But he died in Cairo in November 1290, so his son, Khalil, continued his father's work. A huge army of about 200,000 marched from Egypt to Acre, while the crusaders were able to muster less than 20,000 defenders. The Christians were outnumbered more than ten to one.

The confrontation started with a face-to-face meeting of delegations from the city and Khalil. If the city was handed over immediately, everyone could leave with their possessions. It was a fair offer, but the Christians refused. Then, probably by accident, a catapult from within the city fired a boulder over the walls, landing close to Khalil's tent. Furious at this apparent trickery, Khalil was about to behead the delegates when one of his generals stopped him, realising it must have been fired in error. The end result was an impasse and siege became inevitable. Henry II prepared to lead the defences of the city against this massive army.

Acre had been the site of a number of other epic sieges in the Crusades, and its massive double walls ensured that, while the Crusader force was small, it was extremely well defended. In addition, the defence force was dominated by the military orders, and they were some of the best-trained and best-equipped warriors Europe had to offer.

However, as the size of Khalil's army shows, the Mamelukes hadn't undertaken this campaign half-heartedly. In fact, one great siege engine which had helped to destroy the walls of Crac des Chevalier had been dismantled, placed in 100 wagons and transported over 100 miles to be used once more against another set of Christian fortifications. It seemed Khalil had left nothing to chance.

The crusaders themselves had their own catapults and mangonels (another catapult-type siege engine); and as the Mamelukes began to rain down death and destruction on the Christians, the defenders of Acre returned the compliment. This was April of 1291.

The Christians gathered a small fleet of armoured galleys and sailed out to harass the Mameluke forces camped by the coast. Archers and catapults fired relentlessly on the Muslim camp, making the siege a nasty experience for the Mamelukes as well as the Christians.

Without any apparent hope of reinforcements, the only tactic left to the Christians was to cut off the head of the serpent. The army would have to retreat if Khalil were to be killed. They knew he was not popular with the ethnic Turkish troops in the Mameluke ranks, and it was likely that if he were to be killed there would be enough dissent and confusion that the army would retreat to settle its leadership dispute.

The Templars picked a team of their best warriors and sneaked into the Muslim camp at night. But after getting entangled in tent ropes, the would-be assassins were discovered. One poor man tripped and fell into a camp latrine, where he was rapidly dispatched.

By early May some of the towers of Acre had been damaged enough to lead to collapse. By mid-May, Khalil felt he was in a strong enough position to order an all-out assault on the walls. The Mamelukes charged at the ruined walls, accompanied by 300 musicians, their trumpets and drums slung onto the backs of hundreds of camels. The resulting cacophony (for it was hardly music) was meant to encourage the attackers and scare the defenders.

The crusaders met them on the walls and fought ferociously. Throughout the day the advantage shifted backwards and forwards. No quarter was asked and none was given. By nightfall the Christians were still hanging on, while the Mamelukes regrouped under the cover of darkness.

It was at this point that Henry II left for Cyprus with his 3,000 troops. Henry could be accused of cowardice; a captain should go down with his ship. But it was a lost cause. To lose the leader who still ruled Cyprus, as well as a city that had all but fallen, would have been pointless. Besides, he had, for over a month, carried out an energetic defence against overwhelming odds, with no assistance from Europe. Henry was no coward.

The next morning, Khalil noticed a weakness in part of Acre's defences. He ordered the ditch to be filled so that the Mameluke cavalry could gain entrance. Some of Khalil's most zealous soldiers actually threw themselves into the ditch, sacrificing themselves so the Muslims could quickly take advantage of the weakness and bridge the gap. This gave the Mamelukes the foothold they needed to finally break through the defences of the city.

The Mamelukes were in and the defences were collapsing. By nightfall on this second day of assault, most of the city was Khalil's. The one exception was the mighty complex of the Templars' headquarters. The site was protected by sea cliffs on all but one side. Khalil sent negotiators to get these formidable warriors to surrender. The talks bought the Templar Grand Master enough time to escape with the Templars' treasures, ensuring a colossal amount of gold did not fall into the hands of the enemy.

A settlement was agreed, but when the troops came for the formal surrender, the ill-disciplined Mamelukes attacked the Templars, who responded in kind. The deaths of both Muslims and Christians ensured that there would be no second round of negotiations.

Arrows, crossbow bolts and rocks were hurled at the Mameluke besiegers and the entrenched Templars alike. The fight for these last few crusaders against an entire army was hopeless, but that's what spurred them on. The knights knew that the fall of Acre would be a defining moment in crusader history, and they would not shrink away from their moment. The military orders had been created because of the Crusades, and so the threat the Templars faced was personal, as well as immediate.

Grimly, they faced assaults and bombardment from Mameluke siege engines. The noise, the choking dust and the suffering were immense. The bravery to withstand such an onslaught, knowing that there would be no relief, was the stuff of legend. And yet, day after day, the immense Muslim army failed to crack this last tiny bastion of Christian defiance.

To give you an idea of how fiercely the Templars resisted, with all of its defences and thousands of soldiers, it took forty-three days for Khalil to take Acre; it took a further ten days to defeat 200 Templars. This involved more siege engines breaching the walls, and during the final Muslim assault most of the Templars' structure collapsed. It had been so badly damaged that all of the remaining Templars, and virtually all the assaulting Mamelukes, died in this final bloody act.

Acre was lost, which meant the Kingdom of Jerusalem was no more. For nearly 200 years, Christians had held lands in the Middle East, but that chapter of history was now over ... or was it?

Almost all books about the Crusades end with the fall of Acre in 1291. Must be time for a conclusion and bibliography – and off to the printers it goes. But not so fast. Just as I disagree with the conceit that the story of the Crusades starts in 1095, I also disagree that the Crusades ended abruptly in 1291.

Just because we know that there was no Tenth Crusade doesn't mean that contemporaries knew this.

Without question, the period of at least two generations following the fall of Acre was heavily influenced by the Crusades, both in the East and the West. Without the tumultuous events of the 1290s, it's quite likely that a new empire would never have started.

The Mongols may have been beaten back, but they were not beaten. The 1290s saw the last few years of Kublai Khan's reign; his empire may not have taken the Middle East, but it had been busy conquering what remained of China and had tried twice to invade Japan. The Mongol Empire was by now separated into individual 'hordes', areas ruled by local Mongol warlords. One such area was the Ilkhanate, which covered roughly the modern-day areas of Iran, Iraq and the Caucasus. It was vast, an empire in its own right. The Mongol khan of Ilkhanate in the late thirteenth century was Ghazan.

In 1295, much to the disappointment of European diplomats, Ghazan Khan converted to Islam. The Ilkhanate Mongols from this point onwards may have been ethnically Mongol, but they were Muslim rulers. The Ilkhanate was never overthrown or conquered; it was just absorbed into Persia. Meanwhile, Ghazan, while never a Christian ally to the Crusades, was a warrior, and he was preparing for war with the Mamelukes.

It was a good time to do so as Khalil, the victor of Acre, had been assassinated in 1293 and his youngest son, Al-Nasir

Muhammad, had been installed as sultan. His reign was a roller-coaster ride. He lost power in the mid-1290s but made a comeback in 1299, only to lose power again a decade later. In short, the internal turbulence that always brings empires to their knees was happening to the Mamelukes.

Ghazan sent diplomatic missions to Henry II and the Armenian country of Cilicia (in modern-day south-east Anatolia). He was looking for all the support he could get and the Christians were happy to oblige. With a base in Cyprus, the Christians could raid or land anywhere along the eastern Mediterranean coast in relative safety.

In 1299 Ghazan invaded Syria and captured Aleppo. The Mongols, with their Christian auxiliary force, headed south where, near Homs, they met Al-Nasir Muhammad at the Battle of Wadi al-Khazandar. This forgotten engagement showed that the Mongols were far from a spent force. The Mamelukes were heavily defeated, and Al-Nasir was forced to retreat.

Then, in the winter of 1299/1300, the Mongol army descended on Damascus, which surrendered. It was looking like the Christians had backed the right horse this time. Could Jerusalem be wrested from the uncompromising Mamelukes into the hands of the allied Mongols?

In all the confusion, Henry II, along with the three main military orders, decided on the invasion of Ruad, a small island fort a little north of Tripoli.

In 1300 the force successfully took the island and fort. It then moved on to the nearby town of Tortosa and that, too, was quickly captured. Tortosa was meant to have become a permanent base for further operations; however, a lack of discipline meant the occupation turned into an excuse for looting, and the crusaders were forced to regroup back at Ruad.

The modest plan had largely succeeded. Over the next few years, Ruad's defences were improved while hundreds of troops, supplied by both Henry and the military orders, were brought in.

In the meantime, Ghazan was having insurrection problems in other areas, which led to the delay of any campaigning in the Middle East for a few years.

This period of inactivity allowed the Mamelukes to attack Ruad in 1302; but after failing in its assault of the island, they surrounded it with their fleet, intending to starve it into surrender. The defenders eventually had no choice but to capitulate. Once again the Templars were offered the chance to leave a defensible position unmolested, and once again Mameluke troops broke the promise and a fight ensued. The defenders of Ruad were either killed or enslaved, but, as on other occasions, the Mamelukes had found the Templars to be obstinate and determined enemies.

A year later, Ghazan was again ready to push into Syria. He sent his general Qutlugh to lead the army, and yet again the Mongols met the Mamelukes in battle. This time the Battle of Marj al-Saffar went the way of the Mamelukes.

Like Ayn Jalut, the losses on both sides were heavy. Yet again, the deciding factor was the death of the Mongol general. After Qutlugh was killed in the battle, the Mongols were forced to retreat. It was a decisive, but not humiliating, defeat for the Mongols. As it turned out, this was to be the last Mongol invasion of the Middle East. With the fading of the great khan lineage, the Mongol warlords were to spend decades fighting each other rather than making further conquests.

The late thirteenth and early fourteenth centuries were a time of tumultuous change in the Middle East. Byzantium had become a shadow of its former self, but was back in its seat of power at Constantinople. The Italian traders were vying for control at every port on the Black Sea and Mediterranean. The Christians had lost their base on the mainland but still held Cyprus. Finally, the Mongols and

Mamelukes were wracked with internal feuds. Meanwhile, a band of warriors was making the most of this churning chaos.

Three hundred Turkish horse archers, led by Osman, had been mercenaries for hire for years. As almost everyone wanted and needed more troops, business was good. It's alleged that one night Osman had a strange dream in which a great tree grew out of his navel as he lay there in the shade. He wanted to know what it meant and was told that he would found a great empire. This is almost certainly later propaganda, but it's worth noting that had the 1290s not been so turbulent, Osman would have ended up as just another horse archer, much like tens of thousands of others, utterly forgotten by history.

But Osman knew how to make the best of a bad situation. His father had fled to Anatolia in the mid-thirteenth century to avoid the onslaught of the Mongols. In the process, he had managed to capture the small Byzantine town of Thebasion and renamed it Söğüt.

After his father's death in 1281, Osman was confirmed head of the town by its Seljuk overlords. But this success was little more than a toehold. In the big scheme of things, the crusader base of Ruad was of greater significance to contemporary Muslim powers than Söğüt. However, it is to Osman's credit that he recognised the status quo was changing; under the circumstances, a man with ambition (and a small army) could make something of himself. Osman and his descendants were to fight not just against the ailing Byzantine regime but against other Turkish princes in Anatolia. With such an inauspicious start, any major reversal could have ended his empire-building before it even began. But Osman proved to be a competent military leader, carefully picking his battles and leaving a secure, if modest, stretch of lands for his son Orhan. The son continued his father's tactics of cautious expansion from 1326 onwards.

Osman is the Turkish variation of the Arabic name Othman, and it's by this name (Ottoman in English) that his family and an empire were to become known. The end of the Crusades in the Holy Land saw the start of the Ottoman Empire, which would last until after the First World War.

The Muslims had won the war in the East, and just as the old enemies were fading away, a new enemy, the Ottomans, was rising. Within a generation, they would be striking into Christian eastern Europe.

But all of this was yet to come; in the meantime, there was the question of the military orders, those hugely powerful organisations whose whole point was to go on crusade. With the loss of the Holy Land, they were looking rather pointless.

The Teutonic Knights had always been minor players in the politics of the Middle East, a factor which probably saved them; they still had plenty of campaigning to do in northern and central Europe. Over time, as their enemies converted, there were fewer and fewer pagans, but more and more Eastern Orthodox Christians. As far as the papacy was concerned, feuding with Russia, a semi-barbaric country full of Orthodox heretics, was fine.

And so it was left to the two largest military orders to confront their own reason for existing. After all, the point of these organisations was to protect pilgrims in Palestine and to wage holy war against the infidel. That had just come to an abrupt halt. Now Europe was hosting the Hospitallers and Templars, two hugely wealthy organisations that answered only to the Pope. And they had nothing to do.

13

Betrayal: Final Crusading Plans and the Templar 'Heresy'

The Templars were like an army in search of a war. They had men, land, resources and a huge amount of money which only they had access to. But their riches made them vulnerable; a worrying position at a time when the papacy was close to bankruptcy and most of their lands were in France, which was also broke. The Templars were starting to look like an easy target.

The origins of the idea that Friday the 13th is an unlucky day are hard to prove; however, it is widely thought that the next part of the Templars' story could be the source. In September 1307, King Philip IV of France sent secret documents to all the bailiffs and seneschals (stewards in charge of medieval estates), ordering preparations to be made for the arrest of all members of the Knights Templars. These arrests were carried out on Friday, 13 October.

The sealed orders began like this:

A bitter thing, a lamentable thing, a thing which is horrible to contemplate, terrible to hear of, a detestable crime, an execrable evil, an abominable work, a detestable disgrace, a thing most inhuman, set apart from all humanity.

This is not how most arrest warrants start and shows how

Philip needed to win over his own bailiffs for this plan to work.

The trial of the Templars is one of the most shameful chapters in both French and papal history (and there have been a few). In truth, it is so bizarre that this historically confirmed event has led to a number of conspiracy and crackpot theories. Writers of present-day fiction like to claim that it was all done to cover up the true bloodline of Jesus, but there is no mention of any of this in any of the medieval chronicles. It's modern myth making.

The reason for this trial was simply a need for money, and the fact that the Templar institution was redundant. With the end of the Crusades, Europe didn't need these huge military orders ready to fight in the Middle East. It could just as easily have been the Hospitallers who were victimised, but it wasn't.

Heresy is a crime prosecuted by Church courts, so the king could not arrest people on such a charge. However, because of the French throne's interactions with the Albigensian Crusade, the French king did still, technically, have this authority simply because the papacy had never bothered to revoke it.

Papal history is one of the most complex topics in all of history, so this is a brief summary of the relevant events. With the backing of Philip IV, the new Pope, Clement V, had only just managed to win enough support to become Pope. Clement was, therefore, greatly indebted to the French king and obliged to help Philip with his brutal plan to dismantle the Templar organisation. So while the French king's authority in heresy cases was technically to do only with a specific crusade (which had taken place nearly 100 years earlier), Clement was never going to point this out.

Heresy was a convenient way to attack the Templars. After all, they hadn't tried to overthrow the French monarchy or done anything particularly illegal. In fact, because the

Templars had invented an early form of banking (and the cheque), they were working in King Philip IV's treasury and were never seen as anything other than completely trustworthy ... until the autumn of 1307. While they were now an unemployed army, they had nearly two centuries of legendary achievements behind them. Their bravery at the fall of Acre and, more recently, at Ruad was still fresh in peoples' minds. It was a high-risk strategy (hence the dramatic opening to the sealed orders).

But heresy is like a plague; start tarnishing someone's reputation with such a crime and nobody will leap to your defence, in case they might also become tainted.

Jacques de Molay had become Grand Master of the Templars in 1293. He had been in the Holy Land from 1270 to the fall of Acre. By 1307 he was an old man, but despite his age he was still coming up with new ideas.

Early in 1307, he had sent a letter to the Pope with suggestions about how the three main military orders could be merged. While this shows that he was willing to think laterally, it was also an acknowledgement that the reality on the ground had shifted and that it might be time to do something about the structure of the military orders. Perhaps most importantly, it showed that the Hospitallers, the Templars and the Teutonic Knights weren't all that different. This is something to remember as conspiracy theory, heaped upon hearsay, exaggerated by lurid pseudo-history, has made the Templars seem far more exotic than the other military orders. They weren't. They just had the bad luck to be in the wrong place at the wrong time.

Another letter from the same time showed that Molay was planning a modest crusade to the Holy Land. Again, the letter is realistic: too large a request for troops and the endeavour will never take off; too small and there's no point in doing it. The Grand Master was relatively attuned to the politics of the early fourteenth century.

The fact that the Grand Master of the Templars, along with scores of other men, was grabbed on that fateful Friday 13th is not a sign of naivety. Philip had wanted the strike to come from nowhere, and his plan had worked perfectly. The bailiffs had obviously listened to the king's dramatic words in the letters and stayed silent.

The knights were thrown into prison and the torture began. Meanwhile, the Pope exhorted the remaining Templars not to flee as that would not help their case – and he was sure a solution could be found.

What this suggests is either that Clement was woefully naive or, more likely, that in his mind (and probably Philip's), they could get the accusations of heresy confirmed. This would allow them to get their hands on the Templars' assets, while the Templars themselves would fade away and perhaps be absorbed into monasteries elsewhere. This is speculation, but it's worth pointing out that this case dragged on for seven years, so there must have been a number of plans and changes of heart throughout the proceedings. Had the plan always been to execute them, that could have been done much quicker than a court case that lasted most of a decade.

Philip played the role of a monarch who had been forced to turn against such a noble institution. He claimed he hadn't wanted to act, but that the weight of accusations was so great he had no choice.

The charges were specifically that the Templars' initiation was blasphemy of the highest order and that

> when professing, the brothers were required to deny Christ, to spit on the Cross, and to place three 'obscene kisses' on the lower spine, the navel and the mouth; they were obliged to indulge in carnal relations with other members of the order, if requested; and finally they wore a small belt which had been consecrated by touching a strange idol, with looked like a human head with a long beard.

There was some argument during the case about spitting on the crosses. This seems to be true but was done so that if Templars were captured by Muslims who made them do it, they would feel no revulsion in doing so. The whole 'kissing on the navel' is a medieval euphemism for gay oral sex, an act that can still get conservative authorities hot under the collar, so in medieval France it was pretty much dynamite. It also had the advantage of requiring no evidence. Were there gay Templars? All those men together, close proximity, no access to women, vows of chastity … you decide. But were they a heretical Christian sect that was a threat to papal authority? Definitely not!

The accusations were shocking and so counter to the 200-year reputation of the Templars that even the most naive of contemporaries recognised the whole thing for what it was – a set-up.

Clement himself wavered. In 1308 he stopped the Inquisition from further investigations into the Templar heresy; and in the same year, the Chinon Parchment shows pardons for the leadership of the Templars.

The problem for Clement and Philip was that the Templars kept confessing their sins and then recanting them, saying they had been forced or tortured. In 1310 Clement set up an ecumenical council, not under French authority, to look into both the charges and the future of the Templars.

At any point up until 1310, this whole situation could have been resolved with a minimum of fuss. Indeed, a number of people defended the order, showing that the case was clearly a weak one. In those times, if someone was an obvious and known heretic, there could be further charges against defenders for coming to the aid of a heretic (that's medieval logic for you).

In May 1310, everything changed when Philip had fifty-four Templars, who had admitted to the charges, burnt at the stake. The situation had gone from dangerous to deadly. Jacques de Molay lacked focus and gave no strong leadership throughout all of this; he was out of his depth. As an old man reared on war against the Muslims, he thought he knew whom his enemy was; and yet, here he was, having to defend his beloved order to the King of France – a man descended from crusaders – and the Pope, who should have been the Templars' defender, not their accuser. It was a tricky political situation for the sharpest of minds, so it's little wonder that the old warhorse didn't know what to do.

But this indecision meant the Templars themselves lacked a cohesive defence. Sometimes they would be marched into court, admit to all the charges and face future lives as penitents. Other times, they would change their testimony, meaning they were recanting under oath, a certain sign that they were renewing their heretical beliefs. These men were systematically beaten, starved and threatened. They were held in prison for years, with no knowledge as to when or if they could expect release. And as if all of this was not enough, terrible tortures often awaited them in these dark dungeons of medieval France. The Templars were surrounded, lacked leadership, had taken casualties and had no escape plan. It was as bad as the fall of Acre.

By 1313 Philip was enjoying the spoils of this recent endeavour. He sent envoys to the Hospitallers to complain that he had lost substantial sums to the Templars and request that the Hospitallers reimburse him. The Hospitallers recognised that what had happened to their brother knights could happen to them, though the threat was implied but never stated. The Hospitallers gave Philip 200,000 livres tournois to 'compensate' for his losses. To put that into context, that's half the ransom that was paid for Louis IX when he was captured on the Seventh Crusade. It was a colossal sum, approximately one-sixth of the annual income of the whole of France. But it was better to pay up than to risk potential investigation by a king who seemed to be getting the hang of prosecuting heresy charges against the military orders.

At about the same time, Pope Clement declared that anyone who tried to associate the Hospitallers with the heretical acts of the Templars would face excommunication. One colossal made-up heresy case was obviously enough for both king and Pope.

The money Philip received from the Hospitallers might well have been intended to assuage his guilt, because in 1313 Philip took the cross and promised to go on crusade. But first the trial of the Templars would have to come to a close.

The case reached its tragic conclusion on 18 March 1314. The Grand Master and the other regional masters of the Templars were brought in front of Notre Dame and tied to stakes. Jacques de Molay repeated yet again that the charges against him and all the Templars were false.

He also declared that God would punish the misdeeds of the King of France and the Pope, and that they would both be dead within a year. And with that, the leaders of the Knights Templar were burned. They did not cry out or beg for mercy, but instead died with such composure that afterwards the crowd surged forward and gathered their ashes to be kept as holy relics – hardly a common reaction to burned heretics.

A month after this disgraceful climax to the trial, Pope Clement V died. It is said that as his body lay in state, a lightning bolt struck the church and burned most of his corpse. In November of that same year, Philip IV also died, killed during a hunting trip. Hunts were dangerous, and there have never been any accusations of foul play, so it's safe to conclude that neither was assassinated by fugitive Templars. But Jacques de Molay's prophecy had been fulfilled.

If the deaths of king and Pope were shrouded in mystery,

other questions arose out of the disappearance of the Templars' treasury, for when French officials opened the door it was empty. Obviously a Templar, or someone loyal to them, had made sure nobody else would get their hands on these riches. As a result, this disappearance has been the source of much speculation, but to save everyone the time and effort of wading through semi-history, let me conclude by saying that nobody knows what happened to the treasure. It was never found.

Mysteries to one side, the demise of the Templars is an example of how brutal and amoral medieval Europe could be. Just a generation earlier the Templars had been untouchable, seen as the very embodiment of Christian courage. It all ended on a wooden scaffold in front of Notre Dame Cathedral.

Nobody can put a specific date on when the Crusades ended. Even as the Templar trial was continuing, Philip IV was seriously considering a crusade, as was Jacques de Molay before he was arrested. While other factors must be taken into account when describing the death of the crusading movement, the trial of the Templars was as fatal a blow as the loss of Acre more than twenty years earlier.

While the precise end to the Crusades is difficult to pinpoint, for me, personally, it arrived when Christian Europe got to the stage of attacking organisations that embodied the crusading ideal. No matter how romantic that ideal would become, no matter how much people would want to hark back to past glories, it wasn't just an old man or a military order that burned on that March morning; it was the very concept of Crusade.

The Hospitallers were lucky (and had paid handsomely to be lucky), but realised a new mission was urgently needed or the fate of the Templars might also be theirs. So, at the expense of the Byzantines, they founded a new base of operations when they captured the island of Rhodes in

1309. It was here that they built a fleet designed specifically to harass Muslim sea trade, and the Knights of Rhodes became a major thorn in the side of the Mamelukes, who, in 1444, attempted to besiege and take the island but failed. Later still, in 1480, the Ottoman sultan Mehmet II, the conqueror of Constantinople, also tried and failed to capture this base of persistent and irritating operations. Rhodes was very close to the Ottoman Empire, and it was remarkable (and a sign of how well designed the defences were) that, decade after decade, the knights could attack Muslim shipping with impunity.

The once land-based Hospitallers, with their much-feared heavy cavalry, had become the much-feared Christian pirates of the eastern Mediterranean. Their heavily armed galleys preyed on merchant shipping, Muslim diplomatic missions and even the occasional small fleet. They were, in theory, the first privateers. The reason why Queen Elizabeth I of England allowed English ships to act as pirates against Spanish galleons was because that was the only way England could wage war against the giant empire (and treasury) of Spain. While this was true in the mid-sixteenth century in England, exactly the same could be said for the Hospitallers, who confronted the Muslim empires of the East from the early fourteenth century right through to the Renaissance and beyond.

It would take until 1522 for someone to finally better the knights, and that person was Sultan Suleiman the Magnificent. It was an epic siege, which took a fleet of 400 ships, 100,000 soldiers and five months to finally breach the defences. The struggle so exhausted Suleiman's resources that he allowed the Hospitallers to leave the island with all that they could carry.

After this, the Hospitallers found a new home on the island of Malta, where they continued their piracy. In 1565 Suleiman attacked them again, but this time the giant

Ottoman fleet and army failed to capture the Hospitaller-held island. The knights would continue to rule until Napoleon arrived in the late eighteenth century and forced them to disband.

The Hospitallers still exist as a Catholic charity, but it isn't really the same organisation. However, there is a direct link from the Grand Master of the earliest Crusades, through the Renaissance, to the end of the eighteenth century, right up to today. This is just one lasting legacy of the Crusades.

The Inquisition also flourished for centuries and came to be known, in the late fifteenth century, as the Spanish Inquisition. The trials lasted longer than you might think; the last Inquisitorial trial was in 1826, when a teacher was found guilty of teaching 'deism' and was executed. The Inquisition, like the Hospitallers, adopted more moderate attitudes with age and, as mentioned earlier, is now known as 'the Congregation for the Doctrine of the Faith', a body which advises the Pope on specific points of Catholic doctrine. Nobody gets burned anymore.

For generations young nobles had gone on crusade, if not on one of the major ones then as part of a small expeditionary force to help garrison some exotic far-off town or castle in the Holy Land. And later, when the opportunities in the East had faded, the routine of blooding yourself on crusade had not. Instead, we see the princes of Europe going on crusade with the Teutonic Knights in northern Europe (such as Henry Bolingbroke, the future Henry IV of England). Or if you preferred sun and a Muslim enemy, there would be an opportunity for another 200 years (until the last Muslim prince was defeated in 1492) to campaign on the Iberian Peninsula. Robert the Bruce, King of Scotland in the early fourteenth century, wanted his heart to be taken on crusade when he died. His donated organ was sent to Spain.

In essence, the same concept of packing your bags and

getting a campaign under your belt in faraway countries still existed; and it was much easier for a nobleman to get from England to Germany or Spain than it ever was to go all the way to Palestine. The principle was the same, but now an unspoken realism had crept in: yes, Jerusalem should be Christian; but it was too far away, too lost, to be a serious target for any European campaigning.

The core reason for all this yearning was linked to the highly emotive concept of pilgrimage to Jerusalem, the holiest place in the Holy Land. In 1370 the Kingdom of Cyprus negotiated a deal with the Mamelukes to allow safe passage for Christian pilgrims. This, in turn, led to a highly lucrative tourist trade. At the same time, Philip of Meziers was churning out retrospective histories of the Crusades, which were enormously popular. King Henry V of England and all his European contemporaries might never have gone on a crusade to the Holy Land, but they would have known of the siege of Antioch, Richard the Lionheart and the fall of Acre. They probably pined to do something similar, but now Europe had a Muslim foe much closer to home – and one that was much more dangerous.

In some ways the trial of the Templars marked the close of the crusading movement better than the fall of Acre, but the idea was not done completely.

Although there was a huge amount of bloodshed in Europe from the 1090s to the 1290s, in general the status quo was maintained. But looking ahead from the 1290s to the 1390s, there are the beginnings of a permanent shift in the European power dynamic. In 1340 King Edward III of England declared his claim to the French throne. The French king disagreed, and thus began the so-called Hundred Years War. It was an on/off period of hostility that lasted into the mid-fifteenth century, during which time there was no way either England or France was going to go on crusade.

It was around this time (the 1340s) that the Black Death

arrived in Europe. It is estimated that between a third and a half of Europe's population was wiped out within a couple of years. In times like these, Europe did not have the manpower to waste on a foolhardy expedition to the Holy Land.

It was also about this same time that the Ottomans went from being another minor principality to a genuine threat. As the creaking Byzantine Empire collapsed in slow motion, Ottoman armies started moving into Eastern Europe.

Coalitions and alliances of Christian troops were formed to try and stem the rising tide of Muslim dominance in the Balkans. Since Christian and Muslim armies were clashing, these were, in a sense, crusades, but the key fundamental difference was that all the Crusades were offensive; the fighting occurred in someone else's lands. This time the Christians were the defenders.

In the 1380s we see some reversals for the Ottomans, which led to the epic Battle of Kosovo. In this meat grinder of a battle, a coalition of Christian Balkan princes fought bravely against the Ottoman sultan, Murad I.

The story of the battle is similar to many engagements during the Crusades; the Muslims used their superior archers to start thinning out the Christian troops. The Serbian Christians responded with a heavy cavalry charge that destroyed the Ottoman left flank, but the rest of Murad's army held, and the fighting became a close-quarters melee.

This battle had an unusual twist. A supposed Christian defector was brought before Murad, but it was a ruse and the nobleman managed to plunge a dagger into Murad's stomach before being hacked to pieces by his Ottoman bodyguard. In the long history of Ottoman sultans, this was the only time one was killed in battle (although his son, Beyazid, would become the only Ottoman sultan captured in battle).

Both armies retreated from the battlefield. While the losses were extremely heavy on both sides, the Ottomans could afford to lose troops and the Serbs couldn't. The cream of the Christian soldiers of the Balkans lay dead on Kosovo's soil, but the Ottomans could quickly raise another army; and so it was that, year after year, the Muslims pushed ever further west.

Going ahead a few generations, the young Sultan Mehmet II besieged Constantinople, which fell in 1453, bringing an end to the Byzantine Empire. There had been no crusade to come to the aid of Constantinople's beleaguered citizens, and this Ottoman victory became a symbol of Islamic power in Europe.

A few years after the fall of Constantinople, Pope Pius II issued yet another papal bull, this time giving tax rights and spiritual indulgences to men who went on crusade against the Turks. It came to nothing.

While the Ottomans' superior artillery won the day for Muslim power in eastern Europe, the same technology was to be the downfall of Islam in Spain. Queen Isabella and King Ferdinand had unified Castile and Aragon in opposition to the Muslim state of Grenada. This final war of Christian conquest on the Iberian Peninsula lasted from 1482 to 1492, during which the northern European artillery helped to tear apart previously invulnerable citadels. The war culminated in the eight-month siege of Granada. In certain aspects, this siege mirrored the siege of Constantinople. While both were protracted and bitterly contested, neither ended in massacre. In both cases the cities had little realistic chance of being relieved by a friendly army. Further, each city had been a centre of culture for centuries; and in both cases, their legacies would be deliberately wiped out.

The Ottomans turned the cathedral of Hagia Sophia into a mosque, and the Christians of Spain turned the huge mosque of Cordoba into a cathedral. Subsequently, Spain became one of the most Catholic countries in the world. The Christian conquest of a land where some parts had been Muslim for over 700 years was complete. To put that into context, some areas of southern Spain have still, in the twenty-first century, spent more time under Muslim rule than Christian.

But this final century of conquest in Spain was not really a crusade; it was the dynasties of Aragon and Castile fighting wars of expansion. The Pope may have approved of the war, but troops were not flooding in from France, Germany, Italy or England.

The Christian conquest of the Iberian Peninsula started before the Crusades and ended after the crusading movement had ceased to be active. However, during those 200 years, the Iberian kingdoms aligned themselves with those principles and were rewarded for it.

Two decades later, the Reformation shattered Christian unity in Europe. The Pope was no longer the automatic head of the Church. In some ways, the papacy saw this as the Albigensian Crusade writ large. For example, in 1570, Pope Pius V issued the papal bull referred to as *Regnans in Excelsis*. In it, he calls Queen Elizabeth I of England (a Protestant) a heretic and excommunicates her, adding that anyone who would overthrow her (basically, by killing her) would be given the same indulgences as if they had gone on crusade to the Holy Land. So the Crusades had become the equivalent of regicide. The Pope was inadvertently mirroring the Old Man of the Mountains with his fanatical Hashashins. In case anyone was in any doubt, the Crusades had clearly lost their way.

The horrifying religiously motivated violence of the Albigensian Crusade can be seen in the sectarian atrocities of the Thirty Years War. This is when, from 1618 to 1648, the whole of Europe was engulfed in war, murder and destruction, all in the name of Protestant and Catholic versions of Christianity. Rarely has a European war been so bloody and hate-fuelled (and that's saying something). The war was not a crusade, but shows again how a religious aspect can fuel the flames of conflict.

The very last papal bull for crusader indulgences was raised in the 1930s for the Nationalists in the Spanish Civil War. Although that conflict had nothing to do with the concepts preached by Urban II some 850 years earlier, it's interesting to observe that the papacy still thought it somehow relevant.

The Crusades faded away for many reasons, but they have never been completely forgotten. Moments of real history took on the mantle of legend. But no matter how exotic or how improbable events have appeared in the preceding chapters, they all happened. By the time the Crusades had been confined to the history books, millions had died. All because of *Deus Vult* – God wills it.

Conclusion

Pope Urban II's speech at the Council of Claremont was portentous and dripping with fury and rage. He set the tone perfectly for the next 200 years of conflict. And for those 200 years (or so), Christian armies fanned out into northern Europe, southern Europe, North Africa and the Middle East. After centuries of being under attack, Europe was on the offensive.

With hindsight, the most successful crusade was also the first one; the rest seemed to follow a law of diminishing returns, particularly after the Third Crusade. Therefore, after decades of setbacks, is it surprising that the zeal for crusade faded in the West?

What the previous chapters have highlighted, again and again, is the huge scale of the bloodshed. Populations may have been smaller and mass killings might have been harder to commit than today, but even so the twelfth and thirteenth centuries are some of the bloodiest in history. However, it wasn't just the Christians who were responsible for such huge losses of life. The Mongols were the kings of carnage; it was their atrocities which led to the Muslims feeling so vulnerable that the final few decades of conflict between the crusaders and the Mamelukes were the only time in the crusader era when Muslim armies butchered Christian civilians in large numbers.

And yet it wasn't all blood-soaked destruction. The interaction of East and West had numerous positive outcomes. Even on the First Crusade, there was dialogue between the crusaders and Muslim princes. By the mid-thirteenth century, the military orders were marching with Muslim armies against a common foe.

The Kingdom of Jerusalem, along with the other Crusader States, provided a secure base for the Italian trading powers of Venice, Genoa and Pisa to spread Eastern luxuries to the West. Pepper, silk and ginger all became popular as tastes picked up in the Holy Land were brought back to Europe and regarded as fashionable.

Humble Middle Eastern inventions revolutionised Europe. As unbelievable as it sounds, the wheelbarrow was unheard of in Europe in the eleventh century, and once brought back it was rapidly adopted. Vellum (calf skin) was an extremely expensive way to fill books with pages; the crusaders brought the cheaper 'paper' back to Europe.

Higher learning improved. Many of the ancient Greek philosophers had been forgotten in the West, but it was Arabic translations of these Greek tomes that were then translated into Latin for Western scholars to digest.

Castles were critical in the Holy Land, and their construction made them masterpieces of medieval defensive design; curtain walls and concentric layouts were also brought back to Europe. Monster castles such as Chateaux Gillard (built by Richard the Lionheart) and Beaumaris Castle (built by Edward I) bore designs that had plainly evolved from lessons learned in the Middle East.

While the Christians learned much from their Muslim foes, the Islamic civilisations learned siege craft and how to fight fanatics in return. Europe may have lost Outremer to Islam, but overall Europe benefitted. The Middle East got far less out of the exchange. It seemed that every generation or so, a Christian army would arrive from nowhere and attack key Muslim locations. Is it surprising that, in the East, the term 'crusader' became synonymous with cruelty, death and destruction?

Today, fanatics on both sides point to the Crusades as proof that Islam and Christianity were meant to collide. This belies the complexities of events during the Crusades. Yes, there were huge levels of bloodshed; but just as Europe would regularly explode in bitter feuds between Christian and Christian, the same thing happened between the Muslim princes of the Middle East. Everyone became a soldier of God when it suited them, but day-to-day realities came first. Saladin, the great ghazi fighting against the invading Christian crusaders, actually spent more of his reign fighting fellow Muslims than foreign Christians.

At the end of the Sixth Crusade, a Muslim ruler negotiated the handover of Jerusalem to Frederick II. Negotiated solutions occurred far more often in crusader history than most people think. This was particularly true of the later ones.

Referencing the Crusades to make a point about modern politics is like saying the Battle of Hastings is relevant to EU foreign policy. It's ridiculous, and trying to distil these past events into good versus evil, or using an 800-year-old massacre to justify modern atrocities, is mendacious.

Look at it this way: if zealous crusaders could compromise with the medieval mujahideen, if these two ideologically antagonistic sides could reach agreements and have cordial relationships with each other, then why can't we do the same today?